The X-Craft Raid

Other books by Thomas Gallagher

Nonfiction

Fire at Sea: The Story of the *Morro Castle*
The Doctors' Story

Novels

The Gathering Darkness
The Monogamist
Oona O'

Thomas Gallagher

The X-Craft Raid

Harcourt Brace Jovanovich, Inc., New York

First edition
ISBN 0-15-199726-8
Library of Congress Catalog Card Number: 74-153686
Printed in the United States of America
A B C D E

To Walter B. Mahony, Jr., and Robert O'Brien for generosity, help, and encouragement

Preface

"I cannot fully express my admiration for the three commanding officers . . . and the crews of the midget submarines X-5, X-6, and X-7, who . . . in the full knowledge of the hazards they were to encounter . . . penetrated into a heavily defended fleet anchorage. There, with cool courage and determination and in spite of all the modern devices that ingenuity could devise for their detection and destruction, they pressed home their attack to the full. . . . It is clear that courage and enterprise of the very highest order in the close presence of the enemy were shown by these very gallant gentlemen, whose daring attack will surely go down in history as one of the most courageous acts of all times." —*Rear Admiral C. B. Barry, November* 8, 1943

This book, because it is the only one devoted exclusively to the secret World War II mission mentioned by Admiral Barry, deserved, I thought, to be based completely on original sources. I started my research, therefore, in September of 1967, at the British Admiralty in London, where I obtained the three official Admiralty reports of the mission and was kindly offered every assistance by Sir Michael Carey, Second Permanent Under Secretary of State for the the Royal Navy. After many visits to the Admiralty, the Imperial War Museum, Her Majesty's Stationery Office, and the Public Records Office, I interviewed men connected with the development and operation of the British midget submarines, among them George Honour, the midget submarine commander who received the Distinguished Service Cross for the part he played in the Normandy invasion.

From London I went to H.M.S. *Dolphin*, the Admiralty's submarine base at Portsmouth, England, where I went aboard the only British midget submarine still in existence and also interviewed many submariners who had been in the Royal Navy at the time the mission took place. Lieutenant Commander Richard Todd and Lieutenant Alfie Roake were helpful and kind in familiarizing me with the midget submarine, its assets and potential, the risks the commanders and crews faced, and the training they underwent. I would like to express a special debt of gratitude to Commander P. R. Compton-Hall, whose knowledge of midget submarines is equal, if not superior, to that of anyone in Britain.

After visiting Portsmouth I flew to Germany, where, with a German interpreter, Arno Alexy, I traveled by automobile from city to city to interview men who had been aboard the German battleship *Tirpitz* in Kaafjord, Norway, at the time of the midget-submarine attack. In Freiberg I obtained a copy of a "top secret" German document, the *Tirpitz* log, with its minute-by-minute account of what happened aboard the ship on the day of the attack, as well as secret reports signed by Admiral Karl Doenitz, Vice-Admiral Oskar Kummetz, and Captain Hans Meyer, commander of the *Tirpitz.* In Hamburg I spent several hours talking with Captain Meyer, who also gave me his own written account of what happened. From Hamburg I went to Pinneberg, to interview the chief engineer of the *Tirpitz,* Alfred Eichler, a precise man who proved to be an excellent and reliable witness of the sequence of events on the day of the attack. Among the many crewmen interviewed in and around Hamburg and Kiel, I want in particular to thank Admiral Karl Doenitz, Vice-Admiral Oskar Kummetz, and Walter Stube, who gave me their time, even on Sundays, when I'm sure they had other things to do. I would also like to thank my interpreter, Arno Alexy, and Fritz Kamps, who occasionally substituted for him.

In Scotland I met and spent several days with John Lorimer, one of the heroes of the attack on the *Tirpitz.* After giving me his two personal accounts of the many months of training, the secret passage from Scotland across the North Sea to Norway, and the hazardous journey up the Norwegian fjords to the target area, he agreed to travel with me to Kaafjord, in the Arctic, where the attack took place. Even if our trip had been an unfruitful one, Lorimer and I would have found ample compensation in the person of our Norwegian interpreter, Lars Loberg, a tall, warmhearted, wise, and gentle man for whom we soon felt—and still feel—the warmest affection.

As it happened, though, our trip through Norway was far more successful than I had any right to expect. In Tromso I met Alfred Nilsen, a former member of the Norwegian Resistance, who gave me invaluable information about the part the Resistance played in the secret British mission against the *Tirpitz.* Later, on the shore of Kaafjord, we visited the home of Harry Pettersen, one of the three Norwegian agents whose job it was to supply the British Admiralty with information. Pettersen, his father, and many other Norwegian eyewitnesses to the attack were interviewed, both along the shores of Kaafjord and in the nearby town of Alta, where Lorimer was met by newspaper reporters and hailed by the townspeople for the part he played in the midget-submarine attack.

On our return to Oslo I obtained the personal account of the late Torstein Raaby, the Resistance agent who transmitted to London, by means of a secret radio transmitter in Alta, the vital information gathered by Pettersen and the late Karl Rasmussen, the third Resistance agent involved in the midget-submarine operation. In addition, I found in Oslo an old copy of *Aktuelt,* a Scandinavian newspaper, in which the attack on the *Tirpitz* was described by Sub-Lieutenant Richard Kendall, the diver of X-6, the midget submarine on which Lorimer served. Having tried in vain for weeks to locate Kendall in Britain, I was pleased indeed to obtain this translation of his account of what happened.

Back in England, I fortunately located and met, in Titchfield, Mrs. Compton-Hall (Eve Cameron), the lovely and vivacious woman who had been the wife of the late Lieutenant Donald Cameron, the commanding officer of X-6, whose extraordinary bravery during the operation against the *Tirpitz* won him Britain's highest honor, the Victoria Cross. At this point, I had gathered more than enough original material to begin the book, both official documents and personal accounts of those involved in the operation, including the account of Lieutenant Godfrey Place, the commanding officer of X-7 and the only other man to be awarded the Victoria Cross for his contribution to the operation. My research would still have been incomplete, however, without the personal account of Donald Cameron. I therefore want to express my deep and abiding gratitude to Mrs. Compton-Hall, first for giving me so much of her time in her charming home, and second for allowing me to have the personal log that her husband wrote for her and for their son, Iain.

It would be impossible for me to include the names of everyone I met and was helped by during my research, but among those who made important contributions to the mission and those whose generous assistance made my many months of research fruitful I would like to mention the following people. In Great Britain: Robert Alexander, J. C. Atkinson, W. R. Brewster, Joseph Brooks, Don Cameron, Sir Michael Carey, Eve (Cameron) Compton-Hall, P. R. Compton-Hall, W. R. Fell, D. M. Furniss, Edmund Goddard, A. R. Hezlet, George Honour, P. K. Kemp, Richard Kendall, Douglas Kendall, Anthony Land, John Lorimer, Judith Lorimer, John MacCallum, I. S. McIntosh, T. L. Martin, W. S. Meeke, David Moller, J. P. H. Oakley, Peter Philip, Sheila Pike, Godfrey Place, Michael Randolph, Alfie Roake, J. B. Tait, Commander Todd, Cromwell Varley, Captain Wilmot. In France: Yvonne Faurcade, Paul Palmer, John D. Panitza. In Germany: Arno Alexy, Herbert Dube, Alfred Eichler, Fritz Haag, Fritz Kamps, Arthur Mary, Hans Meyer, Karl Ostermeier, Cornelius Ryan, Walter Stube. In Norway: Christian Hauge, Alfred Henningsen, Thorbjorn Johansen, Jan Johassen, Lars Loberg, Erik Myhre, Alfred Nilsen, Astrid Overbye, Harry Pettersen, Sigurd Pettersen, Torstein Raaby, Karl Rasmussen, Tore Regeberg.

Contents

Illustrations

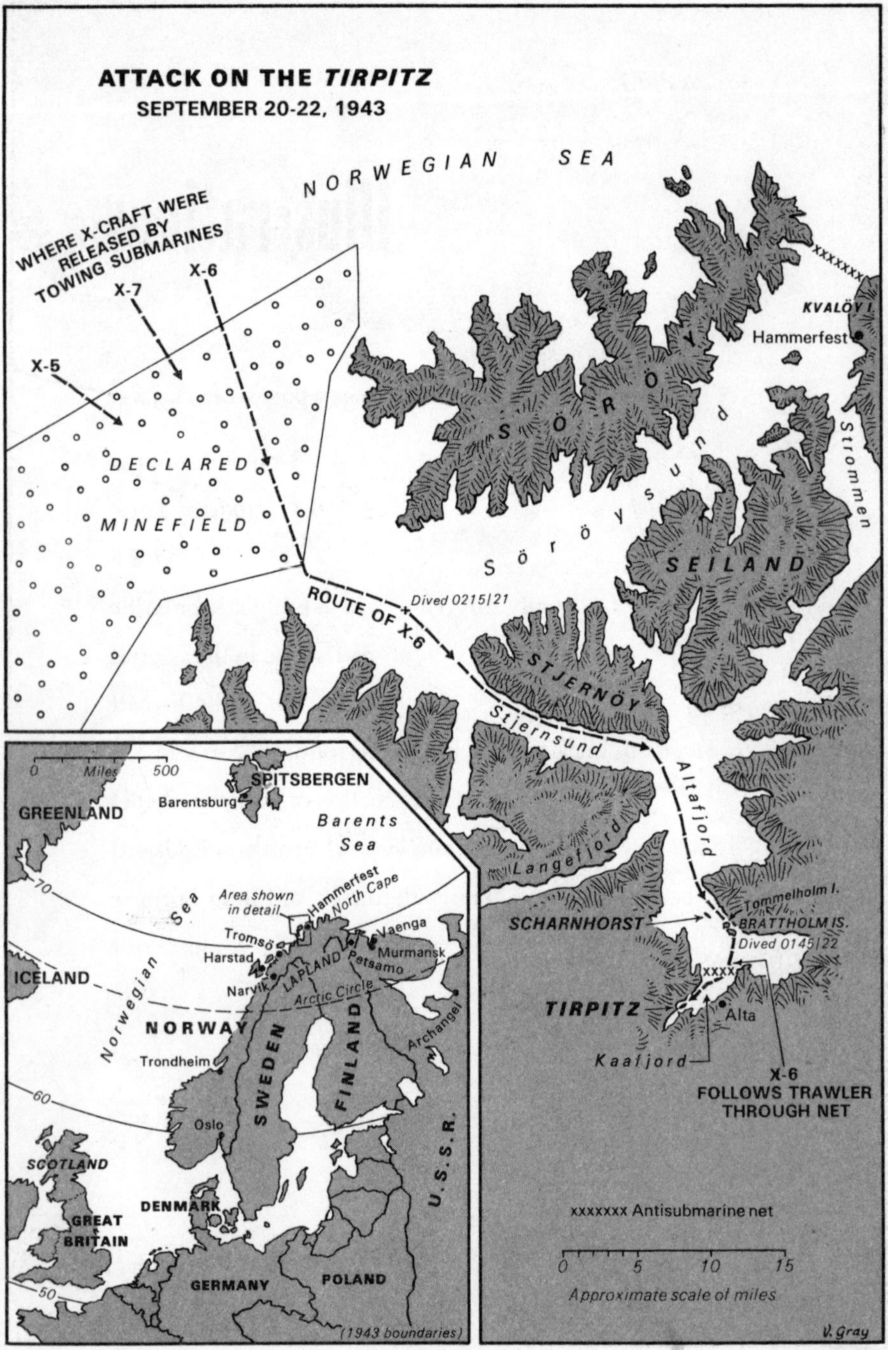

ATTACK ON THE TIRPITZ
SEPTEMBER 20-22, 1943
NORWEGIAN SEA
WHERE X-CRAFT WERE RELEASED BY TOWING SUBMARINES
X-5
X-7
X-6
DECLARED MINEFIELD
ROUTE OF X-6
Dived 0215/21
SÖRÖY
Söröysund
KVALÖY I.
Hammerfest
Strommen
SEILAND
STJERNÖY
Stjernsund
Altafjord
Langefjord
Tommelholm I.
BRATTHOLM IS.
SCHARNHORST
Dived 0145/22
TIRPITZ
Alta
Kaafjord
X-6 FOLLOWS TRAWLER THROUGH NET
xxxxxxx Antisubmarine net
0 5 10 15
Approximate scale of miles
V. Gray
0 Miles 500
SPITSBERGEN
Barentsburg
GREENLAND
Barents Sea
70
Area shown in detail
Hammerfest
North Cape
Sea
Tromsö
Vaenga
Harstad
Murmansk
ICELAND
Petsamo
LAPLAND
Narvik
Arctic Circle
Norwegian
NORWAY
SWEDEN
FINLAND
Archangel
Trondheim
60
Oslo
U.S.S.R.
SCOTLAND
DENMARK
GREAT BRITAIN
GERMANY
POLAND
50
(1943 boundaries)

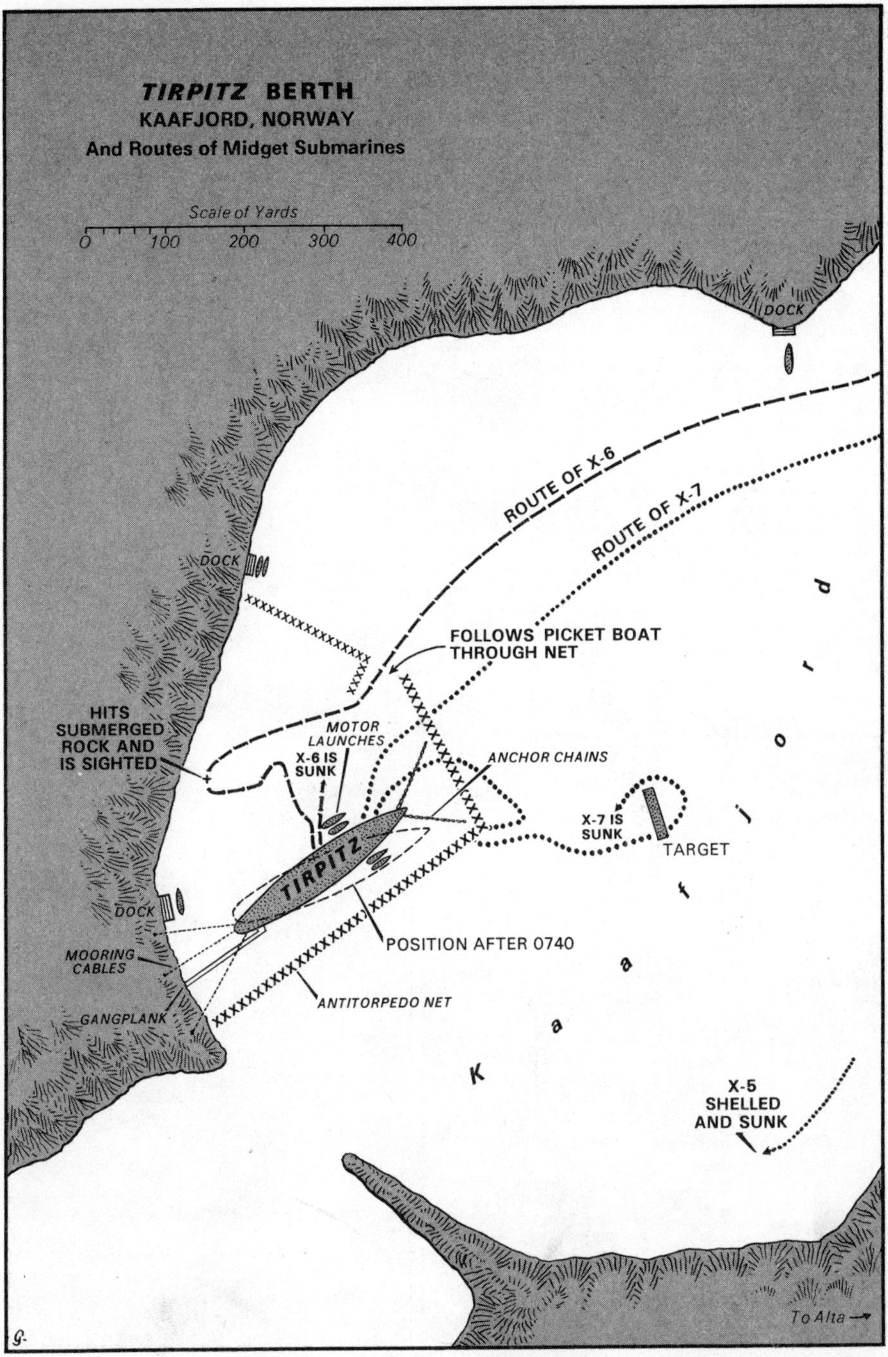

TIRPITZ BERTH
KAAFJORD, NORWAY
And Routes of Midget Submarines
Scale of Yards
0
100
200
300
400
DOCK
ROUTE OF X-6
ROUTE OF X-7
DOCK
FOLLOWS PICKET BOAT THROUGH NET
HITS SUBMERGED ROCK AND IS SIGHTED
MOTOR LAUNCHES
X-6 IS SUNK
ANCHOR CHAINS
X-7 IS SUNK
TARGET
TIRPITZ
DOCK
POSITION AFTER 0740
MOORING CABLES
GANGPLANK
ANTITORPEDO NET
Kaafjord
X-5 SHELLED AND SUNK
To Alta

The Challenge

1

It happened at dawn on Thursday, September 9, 1943. Out of the Arctic Ocean mists off the Norwegian island of Spitsbergen, four hundred miles north of Norway, appeared the mightiest naval vessel in all of Europe. Escorted by a powerful squadron of supporting ships, bristling with guns and the most devastating antiaircraft battery afloat, the German battleship *Tirpitz* had made her approach under cover of darkness and was now ready to strike at this strategically located island.

Before a shot was fired, the Spitsbergen wireless station, high on a hill behind the village of Barentsburg, sent the following message to the Allied wireless station in Reykjavik, Iceland: "Two heavy warships and ten destroyers are approaching Spitsbergen."

Whether it was because of the arctic mists or because Spitsbergen was expecting the arrival of two British heavy cruisers with a strong destroyer escort, the message did not specify whether the ships were British or German. Even so, had the message arrived intact at the station in Reykjavik, the British High Command, knowing its ships could not have reached Spitsbergen, would have had time, with carrier-based planes, to cut off the German naval squadron's escape route back to the safety of Occupied Norway.

The message did not arrive intact, however, because wireless experts aboard the *Tirpitz* interposed Morse signals that made it unintelligible. Meanwhile, nothing had stirred on the island, and apart from the wireless message and the revolving beam from the lighthouse, there was no sign of life.

As the 43,000-ton *Tirpitz* headed straight into the island's main inlet from the sea, Icefjord, she trained her guns on her first target, the wireless station from which the message had been sent. At the same time, the smaller battleship *Scharnhorst* steamed round a spit of land to where military installations lay beneath a coat of snow, while her ten destroyer escorts, carrying assault, demolition, and incendiary squads, raced toward their assigned stations.

Even if the small Norwegian garrison of 150 men had not been taken by surprise, the island's coastal guns would have been no match for the awesome firepower of the *Tirpitz*. Within minutes, the rocky walls of the fjord resounded with the rending flight of shells. There were terrible impacts with earth and jarrings of air, explosive hot flashes in which all the atmosphere seemed concentrated, then moving pockets of smoke over flaming wreckage and fallen men. Struck targets cracked and splintered on their way down, and smoke, flame, and debris erupted from exploding supplies of fuel and ammunition.

The defending Norwegians threw themselves into bunkers and foxholes as stones and flying dirt snapped and ripped at them. Though they fought back with great tenacity, damaging two destroyers and killing or wounding many of the assault troops, their resistance broke down after a third destroyer, covered by the hammering blows of the *Tirpitz*, hauled to a wharf and unloaded its troops.

What followed, as the Norwegians were either captured or forced to retreat into the surrounding hills, was the systematic destruction of everything useful to the Allies on the island. The meteorological station, so important to Allied convoys to Russia, was demolished. Supply depots, military and civilian installations, huge stacks of pit wood, thousands of tons of coal, and whole shiploads of fuel oil were either blown up or set afire. The wireless station, power plant, and waterworks were destroyed by shells; the jetties, piers, and port-loading facilities were wrecked by demolition crews; the coal mines were bombed and the coal pits flooded.

Five hours later, the *Tirpitz,* with several Norwegian prisoners aboard, led her convoy in a swift retreat under a thick cloud of smoke that stretched for miles from the island's burning ruins. Her cruising speed of twenty knots was too fast, the journey back to Norway too short, for the British fleet to intercept her; in fact, the next day, when she re-entered Norwegian coastal waters, the Allied wireless station in Iceland was still trying to establish contact with Spitsbergen. The journey had taken only twenty hours, and now as she neared her home port, she zigzagged her way through her first defense against pursuers—an extensive minefield. Then came the Norwegian fishing town of Hammerfest, the most northerly settlement on the continent of Europe, where a group of islands, separated only by narrow channels, almost completely block the entrance from the open sea. So narrow is one of these channels, the Strommen, between Kvalo and Seiland, that to save transporting them by boat, the herds of reindeer are set to swim across it to take advantage of the summer pastures.

It was here, at the Hammerfest, or northern, entrance to Söröysund, where the islands, Kvalo, Seiland, and Söröy, almost meet, that antisubmarine nets were opened to allow the German naval squadron in. The *Tirpitz,* almost three football fields long, 118 feet wide at the beam, and ten stories high from keel to bridge, slid through with her escorts.

There was little danger now of a surface or underwater attack, for they were entering the Norwegian fjords, those canyons of water that cut deeply into Scandinavia's rugged coast to form an intricate network of rock and ocean. The rock is gnarled and mountainous, with glaciers creeping down its sides, and the water is deep and clear, with enough Gulf Stream water feeding in to make it ice-free the year round. Only in the narrow space between the water's edge and the mountainsides is the land fertile. The people pasture sheep and cattle on it, and eke out a living by fishing.

It is a barren, almost treeless area where more snow falls than melts, where for ten weeks a year the sun does not set and for ten weeks it does not rise, and where during winter storms the only sounds to be heard are those made by the wind. This sweeps in from the southwest off the warm waters of the Gulf Stream, where it is fed an enormous amount of moisture. Then as it rides up the black crags and mountains along the coastline, swirling upward into the colder atmosphere, it disgorges that moisture in the form of snow, snow so thick and blinding that on the ground all sense of an atmosphere is lost.

These storms sometimes last for days. They have prodigious weight and volume and they come in with a steady roar interspersed with rending shrieks like air-raid sirens. Thunderous masses of snow are thrown in whirls and rushes against solitary rocks the size of ocean-going ships, around pinnacles and peaks and into deep crevices and ravines that in time lose all trace of their identity. The entire area becomes inundated in a wildly churning whiteness that separates homes from barns and piles up around lost and isolated sheep until their hair becomes matted with balls of ice, their underbellies weighted down with clumps of ice as huge as those that form under the fenders of cars in winter. Nothing is stable for either feet or eyes to fix upon. Everything moves with the snow's shifting surface or vanishes in the swirling eddies that are ripped off the ground or thrown from the sky by a wind so battering and persistent that even as it races past islands and fjord walls, it seems fastened upon them.

Then, in spring, the currents and whirlpools in the ocean of air above the fjords undergo a dramatic change. The sky turns a turquoise blue; the wind dies down; a cold hush lies over the snow-softened contours of the land. There is everywhere a monstrous kind of harmony between the vast accumulation of snow and what the wind has done to it. Gibraltar-like formations of rock look like icebergs locked in seas of white. The jagged fjord walls are plastered with snow, and high up at the crests of some of them, enormous clumps of snow jut out on the lee side, where the wind-frenzied flakes consolidated with one another. Like huge, pendulous white noses, these clumps of snow reach out into space over the blue waters below, their tons of weight held there by the power of their own cohesion.

It is a lonely, desolate part of the world, one that from the air looks like a vast ink blot. But it is a natural fortress, and the Germans, using science and ingenuity, had made it even stronger.

The gunnery crews at the stern of the *Tirpitz* could see the antisubmarine nets close behind them, the patrol boats probing beneath the surface with their sonar devices, the coastal guns pointing toward the open sea, and here and there, in the town of Hammerfest itself, Luftwaffe fighter pilots on leave from nearby airfields. They knew also that there were antiaircraft batteries in the surrounding mountains, radar stations screening the sky for aircraft, and German occupation troops on patrol to repel Norwegian sabotage attempts.

As the journey inland continued down through Söröysund, the German defense system grew even tighter. Patrol aircraft passed repeatedly overhead, scanning the herring-rich inner waters on the unlikely chance that an English or American submarine had penetrated the minefields off the coast and escaped detection on the way in through one of the entrances. Then came another large, sentrylike island, Stjernöy, and, behind it, Altafjord, or Altenfjord, an always ice-free finger of the sea running twenty miles farther inland. At the end of it was a narrow channel barricaded against intruders by an antisubmarine net hanging from buoys along the surface clear down to the bottom. Made of heavy steel wire and woven into such tight mesh that it could stop a 1,500-ton ocean-going submarine, it was continually floodlit at night and guarded by both patrol boats and shore batteries.

Behind this curtain of steel lay a much smaller body of water called Kaafjord, and it was here—far behind the outer boundary of minefields, shore batteries, patrol boats, Luftwaffe fighter squadrons, antisubmarine nets, and radar and sonar devices—in the most land-locked corner of Kaafjord, 1,000 miles from the nearest air base in Britain but only fifty miles from

Allied convoys bound for Russia, that the *Tirpitz* slowly turned sternward into her covelike berth, a huge, honeycombed fortress of steel in a fjord no larger than a pond.

By location alone she appeared impregnable. But no sooner did the antisubmarine net at the entrance to the fjord close behind her than still another precaution was taken. Antitorpedo nets, made of interlocked nine-inch steel grommets and capable of stopping the largest torpedo traveling at fifty knots, were drawn around her, completely boxing her in, so that her entire hull was protected—on the outside by the nets, and on the inside by the walls of the fjord to which they were attached.

"The Lonely Queen of the North," as her 2,400-man crew called her, was now back in her favorite anchorage, with her stern moored to land, and her bow, pointing toward Altafjord and the open sea, held fast by her port and starboard anchors. All around her the snow-streaked cliffs of the fjord plunged upward to heights that would have made even a carrier-based-plane attack a risky operation. Dive bombers would almost surely have crashed into the walls of the fjord on their upward turn; torpedo bombers, even if they were not destroyed by the flak batteries on either side of their only approach—over the channel from Altafjord—would have had their torpedoes intercepted by the nets around the *Tirpitz* on her water side.

Even the highway, Route 50, running along the opposite shore of the fjord was kept under constant surveillance by the ship's watch. Besides the usual notices—CONTACT WITH THE ENEMY IS PUNISHED BY DEATH—there were signs warning drivers that if they stopped to observe or take pictures of the ship, they would be fired upon without warning.

But the Germans, leaving nothing to chance, had added one final defense to augment all the others. In the surrounding cliffs and mountains, besides the countless antiaircraft batteries, they had placed enough smoke-screen equipment to shroud not only the *Tirpitz*, the *Scharnhorst*, and their destroyer escorts, but all of Kaafjord. Manned on moonlit nights and throughout the daylight hours, the smoke-screen posts were in direct communication with the radar stations along the Norwegian coast, so that they could be put into operation ten minutes before any attacking planes arrived.

These precautions were painstakingly thorough, but even if they all failed, the *Tirpitz* would still be "unsinkable," for tests made in Germany had shown that the special steel hull in which she was encased could withstand the most powerful torpedoes and shells then devised. Sleekly contoured into plates ranging in thickness from five to ten inches, this special steel protected her control center amidships, her power plants, boiler and turbine rooms, her electrical switchboards, gyroscopic-compass rooms, gunnery-control rooms, magazine and shell rooms.

At the water line itself, another belt of steel, six feet wide, was added. It ran from A turret forward to X turret aft, where it thickened to as much as fifteen inches. In addition, the ship's interior, with innumerable steel bulkheads running across and along its entire length, was a veritable labyrinth of passageways and compartments, each one of which could be sealed off from the rest in the event of flooding or explosion. If bombs dropped from high-altitude planes did hit the upper deck, they would explode before reaching the main armored deck that protected this vital interior.

It was no wonder that Admiral Oskar Kummetz, in command of all German naval units in the north, could spend so much time, in breeches and boots, riding a stallion along the shores of Kaafjord. He lived on the *Tirpitz* in a cabin separated from the Captain's cabin by a dining room that he and Captain Hans Meyer, commander of the *Tirpitz*, shared and sometimes used for high-level conferences. Kummetz knew that nothing could happen to the *Tirpitz* in Kaafjord. Until the time came for her to raid an Allied convoy or attack some land installation, she was as safe, as cut off from the war, as a hotel in Switzerland. He could sit at breakfast with the Captain content with the knowledge that since Allied convoys to Russia's arctic ports, Archangel and Murmansk, had to pass through the narrow strip of sea between the north of Norway and the arctic ice, the mere existence of the *Tirpitz* in Kaafjord was holding three to four British battleships and two aircraft carriers from the Pacific, where they were desperately needed.

Yet the broad, flat underbelly of the *Tirpitz*, thirty-seven feet below the water line, *was* susceptible. But who, what, could reach her there, much less with a bomb heavy enough to do any damage?

2

"The greatest single act to restore the balance of naval power would be the destruction or even the crippling of the *Tirpitz*. . . . No other target is comparable to it. . . . The entire naval situation throughout the world would be altered," wrote Winston Churchill in 1942. "The whole strategy of the war turns at this period to this ship, which is holding four times the number of British capital ships paralyzed, to say nothing of the two new American battleships retained in the Atlantic. I regard the matter as of the highest urgency and importance."

Almost from the day in January 1942 when the *Tirpitz* had completed her trials and slipped into Norwegian waters, the British, under Churchill's prodding, had been trying, in vain, to cripple or destroy her. During the first four months of 1942, while she was anchored near Trondheim within reach of land-based bombers in Britain, the RAF had made five separate attempts to destroy her from the air. Fourteen planes were lost, but no hits were achieved.

In 1943, after she had moved to the fjords in the north out of reach of land-based British bombers, Churchill wrote to Premier Stalin, "The Germans have concentrated [in the Arctic] a powerful battle fleet consisting of *Tirpitz, Scharnhorst, Lutzow,* one cruiser, and eight destroyers. This danger to Russian convoys which I described to you last year has been revived in even more menacing form. I explained then that if one or two of our . . . battleships were to be lost or even seriously damaged while *Tirpitz* remained in action, the whole command of the Atlantic would be jeopardized. . . ."

Clearly, the *Tirpitz* could no longer be allowed to bask in the safety of Kaafjord, where she enjoyed all the advantages of selecting her moment to strike without the strain of being always ready to do so. She had to be attacked, and it was unrealistic, it was unmilitary, to wait until she was outside Norwegian waters to attack her.

Besides, the Admiralty knew that despite her tremendous firepower, she would never come out to challenge battle. She might make raids on Allied convoys bound for Russia, but her principal value in Norwegian waters lay in her capacity to make these raids—in short, in her ability to force the Royal Navy to guard every Russia-bound convoy with a squadron stronger than any she could lead in a surprise attack. British cruisers and destroyers were not enough; their armor was no good against her big guns, and they would be destroyed before they could get her within range of their own guns. This meant that at least two battleships of the *King George V* class had to be kept ready to put to sea the moment word reached the Admiralty, from either the Norwegian Resistance or carrier-based reconnaissance planes, that the *Tirpitz* had left or was leaving her anchorage.

"While that damn ship is afloat she will be a constant menace to all our shipping," Churchill kept telling the Lords of the Admiralty. "We must destroy her or seriously damage her."

Later, in a note to Admiral Sir Dudley Pound, First Lord of the Admiralty, he revealed how much the mere existence of the ship annoyed him when he said, "Is it really necessary to describe the *Tirpitz* as the *Admiral von Tirpitz* in every signal? This must surely cause a considerable waste of time for signalmen, cipher staff and typists. Surely *Tirpitz* is good enough for the beast."

Some offensive action had to be taken against the "beast" in her very anchorage in Kaafjord. But how were they to penetrate her elaborate defenses? With what kind of weapon and how many men? It was a problem as old as warfare itself, the kind of problem that has intrigued military strategists ever since the Trojans allowed a wooden horse full of Greek soldiers within their city's walls.

For almost three years, long before the RAF began without success to attack the *Tirpitz*, Royal Navy engineers had been working on a new kind of "Trojan horse," one that would enable a few dauntless men to pass undetected through the various German defense systems, place bombs under the *Tirpitz* in her own anchorage, and escape undetected before the bombs exploded.

From the beginning, these experts agreed that only a submersible of some kind, a submarine in miniature, could meet such a mission's requirements. She would have to be small enough to cross minefields that even at high tide were only fifteen feet beneath the surface. This meant she would have to have a maximum diameter of considerably less than fifteen feet. But despite this size limitation, she would have to be strong enough to dive to depths of three hundred feet, powerful enough to cripple or destroy the strongest battleship in Europe, and versatile enough to avoid detection, cut through antisubmarine nets, and if necessary travel submerged for as long as thirty-six hours. Unlike the various breeds of midget submarines already used in the war, such as the Japanese torpedo launchers, the British and Italian Chariots and Human Torpedoes, and the German Newt, Beaver, and Seal craft, she would have to be launched a long way from her target and have a range of at least three hundred miles, be independent in the operational area and able to overcome such unforeseen circumstances as a last-minute change in plans, an unfavorable tide, or an error in intelligence reports.

The British had been fighting submarines for years. They had used every resource of science—active and passive sonars, echo and magnetic devices—to help solve the problem of detecting a vessel one hundred to three hundred feet beneath the surface. And because of Nazi submarine power, they had the most extensive experience in, and the most advanced knowledge of, antisubmarine warfare. Now they had to put that experience and knowledge in reverse, to avoid detection and secure immunity from attack. They knew that, since German precautions in Norway were directed against full-sized submarines with sufficient range to reach Kaafjord from England, their chances of success and evasion would be much greater with midget submarines. A magnetic detection device sensitive enough to react to the large submerged mass of a full-sized submarine, for example, was also sensitive enough to react, however vaguely, to such trifles as shoals of fish, masses of seaweed, or even cold currents of fresh water. The tiny bulk of a midget submarine was just such a trifle, so that although it would show up on the screen, the operator, trained as he was to make "judgment calls," would, it was hoped, pass it off as a large fish, or a tightly packed school of herring—one of those slight reactions that cause a false alarm a dozen times a day.

The construction and testing of a new type of vessel inevitably results in suggested improvements from both the theorists and the practical sailors. Her speed is too slow, her hull not stout enough, her seaworthiness doubtful. A larger engine would increase her speed, a greater water displacement would enable her to carry heavier armament. Every improvement makes her a better ship, but every improvement also makes her a bigger ship.

With the midget submarine, Admiralty experts were faced with a problem that curtailed experimentation on the one hand and stimulated improvisation on the other. Modifications and improvements could be made only if they fell within the limits of the vessel's required dimensions. At the same time, her armor, equipment, speed, and displacement had to be equal to the task of getting her to the target with explosives heavy enough to destroy the target when she got there. Finally, there was the pressing element of time. She had to be built, tested, and used against the *Tirpitz* before a single Allied battleship was lost or even seriously damaged.

Operating with great secrecy, the Admiralty ordered a prototype midget submarine built by a private company rather than a naval dockyard, and built under the supervision of a man who wore tweeds rather than a uniform. The company was Varley Marine Limited, and the man was Cromwell Varley, the owner of the company, who had conceived the idea of a midget submarine while serving as a Royal Navy commander in the early 1930's.

For weeks, Admiralty officers came down from London to the Varley yard on the Hamble River in southern England. They studied the wooden mock-up of the vessel, examined the complicated electrical and mechanical diagrams, and even climbed into the craft to watch the equipment being installed. All agreed she was a masterpiece of improvisation, but some had doubts about whether grown men with the kind of physical strength and stamina needed for such a mission would be able to exist for days inside a hull so jammed with equipment and machinery.

Finally, on March 19, 1942, at eleven o'clock at night and with the utmost secrecy, His Majesty's first X-craft, or midget submarine, designated X-3, slid from her launching cradle into the waters of the Hamble River. From there she proceeded on the surface under her own power, running low in the water like a raft, for she had no conning tower, to what was to be her hiding place for the next several weeks—a specially constructed floating shed with two hulls, between which she was secured, concealed from the eyes of onlookers.

Meanwhile, a call was sent out to newly commissioned Royal Navy officers for volunteers "for special and hazardous duty." It was a phrase susceptible to almost any interpretation by enemy agents, and when the volunteers arrived, they were told nothing except that they had to be good swimmers. They were put through the most thorough physical examination they had ever experienced and were interviewed in depth by experts who knew how to eliminate those with a morbid dread of being under water or in closed and narrow spaces, as well as those in search of notoriety, undue excitement, or the means to commit suicide. Despite the enormous risk of death or capture involved in such a mission, the Admiralty was well aware that only the most responsible and stable men would be capable of successfully carrying it out.

Over the course of the next several months, as volunteers filtered in from various Royal Navy training schools, the accepted men were divided, without their knowledge, into two groups: those to be trained for possible use as divers in connection with the X-craft operation, and those to be trained to operate the X-craft itself. They were then sent, singly or in twos or threes, to the Royal Navy's great submarine base, H.M.S. *Dolphin,* at Portsmouth, England, where they were guardedly told what they had entered and were given the chance to withdraw.

From this point to the end of the many weeks of preliminary tests and training at Portsmouth, the men of one group knew nothing about the men of the other. They were on a huge submarine base anyway, where no one was expected, much less allowed, to know everything. The various exercises and drills, conducted indoors and out, during the day and at night, were accepted by the trainees as things that happen to servicemen during a war.

The divers, with oxygen containers strapped to their backs, trained first in a tank forty feet in diameter and thirty-five feet deep, learning how to go down to the bottom and to walk around and work for a long time under water. After a week of this indoor exercise, conducted under the scrutiny of an instructor who watched them from outside the tank through a huge glass wall, they worked in rubber diving suits in a lake on the island of Halsey, in nearby Portsmouth Harbour.

Day after day they went down some forty feet to the bottom of the lake, where tiny specks of green algae streamed past their goggles as they learned to saw and hammer wood under water, construct and dismantle engines, and cut through antisubmarine nets. Doing these things also provided a test of their physical endurance, for after six weeks they were often required to remain on the bottom, more like fish than people, for as much as six hours at a time.

The lake was one of the fleet's most secret and best-guarded training areas during the war. Even the divers had no idea what trainees at the other end were doing. Nor did they care until one day when, without warning, the entire lake trembled from an underwater explosion. Someone at the other end had thrown a new bomb device into the lake, and though the divers working at the bottom were a good half-mile away, the impact hit them with the force of a sledge hammer. They shot to the surface, shouting and cursing and flailing their arms. It had been a mistake, of course, and it never happened again while divers were in the water.

For those chosen to operate the X-craft, the preliminary training was no less strenuous, and was much more technical and complicated. They, too, went down to the bottom of the training tank, to accustom themselves to the escape apparatus they would be required to use in the event their craft sank or had her seams buckled by a depth charge. In addition, they were given a theoretical course on X-3, a midget submarine they had never seen. They had to learn to operate trim pumps, hydroplanes, and rudders; to charge batteries and start electrical motors and diesel engines; to test electrical circuits and repair machinery; to conn and to navigate by periscope as well as by such navigational aids as gyrocompass readings and carefully timed shaft revolutions.

During these weeks of preliminary training, the men knew that "something big was up," and some even spoke with assumed authority of their being trained to go "battleship hunting." All they really knew, though, was that they were to use a secret weapon, a midget submarine, in enemy harbors. Speculation revolved around the unanswerable question How? Could a midget submarine cross an ocean under her own power? Was she to be carried by a surface ship or cargo plane to a point within her radius of action? Or was she being built in secret in enemy territory within a few miles of where she was to operate?

As training continued and the rumors and speculations increased, there was seldom an evening when someone didn't say, "Never volunteer for anything in the Navy."

3

The first man to volunteer for X-craft duty was a twenty-six-year-old Scotsman named Donald Cameron, a lieutenant in the Royal Navy Reserve and the commanding officer of the original crew of prototype X-3. He had been in the Merchant Navy since he was sixteen, but had joined the Royal Navy in 1939 and served on a transport ship and then in the submarine *Sturgeon.* A shy, pleasant-faced man with a mind well stocked with knowledge of the sea and a voice laced with just enough of the brogue to confirm his Scottish ancestry, he was a pipe-smoker who made his pipe, whether he was lighting it, stuffing it, smoking it, or cleaning it, a friend and companion.

Among those who joined Cameron was another Scotsman, nineteen-year-old John Lorimer, a tall, straight-backed man who thought nothing of walking ten miles without stopping for a rest. He, too, smoked a pipe and, like Cameron, was destined to play a major role in the seemingly impossible mission against the *Tirpitz.*

"I remember the great day when I went down to the yard to see the first, the only X-craft, X-3," Lorimer recently recalled. "We were shown over by Don Cameron, and I remember thinking how incredibly small everything looked and wondering how such a frail craft was expected to cross the North Sea. . . .

"During the next three weeks we went over to the Hamble occasionally, but X-3 spent most of her time in the big shed . . . while Admiralty experts arrived, trying to sell their various instruments, most of which would not even get inside the craft."

Meanwhile, instruction in submarines continued for the volunteers, along with human adaptation and endurance trials. How much heat and humidity could they endure in a rigidly confined space under water? For how long? Would the cramped conditions dull their attention to the myriad gauges, dials, and instruments they would be required to read and operate? Could adjustments be made in the craft itself?

These and many other questions had to be answered while the daily training regimen continued. The men had to sharpen their minds, quicken their reflexes, and work off every ounce of fat. Luckily, they were young, and, partly because of the war and partly because of Hitler's insolence in thinking Britain could be conquered, there was a "fitness craze" both in and out of the services. The volunteers cut trees, walked, ran, exercised —drove themselves until their abdomens were lean and their backs laced with muscle.

As Lorimer put it: "If you are going to do anything dangerous, the best way to accomplish it is to train, train, train, so that in the excitement of the situation you do the thing automatically. I cannot overemphasize the drilling they put us through, the importance of it, the fact that none of us minded. Rank? We were as near the American system as the Royal Navy could get. We lived like pirates, called one another by our Christian names, but the discipline was complete. When an order was given, it was immediately carried out."

The growing *esprit de corps* among the men was paced by modifications and improvements made in the X-craft during the weeks devoted to her navigation, speed, surface, and diving trials. A great deal of original thinking had gone into X-3; she was a new kind of submarine, and when the volunteers started handling her under service conditions, they were immediately faced with all the unforeseen defects and difficulties that anything new and original always presents. Even standard submarines of proven design startle their crews with their sometimes capricious behavior underwater; with the X-craft, the technique of diving and maintaining a constant depth had to be worked out practically from first principles.

There were tests of battery endurance, of the gyrocompass, of the craft's trim and maneuverability in different densities of water, and of the controls, which were mostly handraulic rather than hydraulic, because the latter would have required too much space.

When all the tests and trials had been completed, and the craft's final design had been approved, top-secret blueprints were rushed to Vickers Armstrong Limited, a shipyard with a large and highly experienced labor force. After the strictest security measures had been imposed and arrangements made for the yard to continue operations day and night, the Admiralty placed an order for six midget submarines to be built.

"As soon as they're ready," Churchill told Admiral Sir Dudley Pound, "we'll try them."

After a fortnight's leave, the volunteers reassembled at a bleak vacated hotel beside the sea in Scotland: the Kyles Hydropathic Hotel, at Port Bannatyne, where in peacetime people with rheumatism partook of the curative properties of the waters flowing through its elaborate basement baths. Situated high on a hill and built of gray local stone that resembled the skin of an elephant, it overlooked the little fishing village of Port Bannatyne and a fjordlike waterway, Loch Striven, from which all nonessential boat traffic had been barred.

"The hotel's carpets and more fragile pieces of furniture were removed," Lorimer recently said. "But the enormous afternoon teas in the mess made up for whatever we lacked in furnishings. We'd sit there and relax, looking out the wide windows across the bay or down at the village and the bend in the loch at the bottom of the hill."

An old shooting lodge stood at the head of the loch, and this, too, was requisitioned by the Admiralty, to serve as an advance base for the X-craft volunteers. Life there was much more informal and rural, with cows, sheep, and poultry grazing outside, home-grown vegetables from a garden in the rear, daily milk deliveries from a nearby farm, and long yarns before a roaring fire at night over pints of cellar-cool beer.

When prototype X-3 arrived from Varley Marine Limited by railroad boxcar, followed by prototype X-4, the volunteers, after being given still another chance to withdraw, began the next stage of their training. In command of X-4 was Sub-Lieutenant Basil Charles Godfrey Place, a graduate of the Royal Navy's college at Dartmouth. There is a saying in Britain, where in wartime the Navy is made up of three separate and distinct categories of men, that those in the Royal Navy are gentlemen trying to be seamen; those in the Royal Navy Reserve, seamen trying to be gentlemen; and those in the Royal Navy Volunteer Reserve, yachtsmen or peacetime sailors who are neither or both. Godfrey Place was the only Royal Navy man among the X-craft volunteers, and though he did indeed speak in the well-modulated tones of a gentleman from Mayfair, he was already, at the age of twenty-two, a veteran of the submarine service and holder of the Distinguished Service Cross.

A short, slender, dark-haired, handsome man, he was "sloppy but incredibly cool under pressure," according to George Honour, a diver who had once roomed with him. "One day I found him with bits of machinery all over my bed. His hands were black with graphite and so were my sheets, but if I showed any emotion, he showed none at all. He was brilliant and ambitious, and his reports to the Admiralty were probably carefully and thoroughly done to help forward his career in the Royal Navy. Without a war, a man finds it difficult to attain the rank of captain. He must work to the top before the age of forty-five. With a war, he advances more rapidly—if he survives."

Place was popular with the other volunteers. They liked him for his dry humor and kindness, and after a while they even accepted his odd habit of taking a fancy to another man's boots, hat, shirt, or tie, and wearing it without permission. Anyone missing a favorite piece of apparel knew it would reappear that afternoon at tea, on Godfrey. They all waited patiently until Godfrey took a fancy to something else, then quietly retrieved what was theirs.

One thing that bothered the men at Port Bannatyne was security. They found it difficult to believe that some word of their activities had not leaked through to the Germans, for tourists could stroll along the waterfront without any kind of special clearance. The village was only a mile or so from Rothesay, one of Scotland's most popular holiday resorts, and anyone passing through could see the X-craft moored to their buoys. Had the craft been equipped with conning towers, the most uninformed onlooker would have known they were some kind of submarine. Luckily, their queer shape and low-lying stance in the water made it difficult, if not impossible, to tell what they were or for what they were intended.

The volunteers naturally tried to be as inconspicuous as possible. They never dived, for example, until they had rounded the bend and were out of sight in Loch Striven, and they always returned to their buoys on the surface. Their manner ashore was unmilitary, their attitude toward uniform and rank amiably indifferent. If a townsman or tourist became openly inquisitive, they said they were testing a new type of rough-water motorboat. It was this very casualness that paid off in the end. Security guards and barbed-wire fences would have alerted tourists and residents, and finally German agents as well. But nobody thought twice about boats bobbing at their buoys for all to see, however odd their shape might be.

Not even the commandos training at the other side of the bay from Port Bannatyne had any idea what the X-craft men were doing. One morning, in fact, a newly arrived colonel at the base happened to awake just as Don Cameron, standing on the casing of X-3 with his feet just about the water's level, his body erect, and his pipe in his mouth, passed by at six knots. The colonel had had a rather heavy night with some Scotch-drinking friends, and when he looked out his window and saw a man skimming over the water with no visible means of support, he probably swore off drinking for the duration.

When the X-craft's depot ship, H.M.S. *Bonaventure,* arrived from Portsmouth and anchored far out around the bend in Loch Striven, it became a more popular rendezvous for the volunteers than either the hotel, the shooting lodge, or some pub in town. She had huge derricks that could lift the X-craft out of or into the water, and she was broad-beamed, roomy, and comfortable enough to give the X-craft men, after a cold, wet, greasy day at sea, an exquisite sense of security and warmth. Hot baths and showers, man-sized towels, and relaxation over a pint of beer were the order of the day aboard *Bonaventure,* as were well-cooked, hot meals served at long tables covered with really white tablecloths. The X-craft men valued these unexpected touches of civilized living aboard their squat and doting mother ship, and did all they could to preserve them. She represented some of the small peacetime pleasures that one misses only after war takes them away.

Yet as the training period stretched on with no end in sight, boredom, discouragement, and frustration set in. The volunteers did the same thing over and over again; they tested the same equipment, dove and surfaced in the same water within reach of the same auxiliary ships, watched the same shoreline slip by through their periscopes, and saw the same faces at sea and ashore.

To become lax and inattentive during these daily tasks would have been easy had it not been for the image of the *Tirpitz* looming in their minds. They knew the time was coming when they would have to penetrate enemy waters and attack the prize of the German fleet in a way that no battleship had ever been attacked before. This shared knowledge during their daily regimen, as they lay in their bunks at night, and even in the evening, when they often sang a wide range of songs and sometimes behaved riotously, did not dispel the extreme monotony of their training. In fact, it added to its devastating psychological effects.

There were many minor training mishaps but no serious accidents until one day in November.

John Lorimer, in command of X-3 at the time, was taking Sub-Lieutenants Gay and Laites out on a trial run. When they went around the bend of Loch Striven to the exercise area and proceeded to dive, water began rushing into the craft through the induction trunk, an air vent used for cruising on diesel power at periscope depth.

"The induction trunk had been closed," Lorimer later explained, "but not tightly shut, due to a piece of foreign matter getting between the valve and its seat."

As water poured into the control room, the craft took a bow-up angle of eighty-five degrees and started slowly sinking stern first. The men grabbed pipes and fittings, in an effort to maintain their balance, and went to work.

"Blow the main ballast tanks," Lorimer said.

This would have compensated for the water pouring in and sent the craft back to the surface. But one of the sub-lieutenants, slipping on the wet deck boards, because of the craft's bow-up angle, dropped the wheel spanner into the bilges. Without it there was no way to blow the ballast tanks, and to retrieve it they would have to unbolt the deck boards from the craft's steel framework—a ten-minute job at least.

Meanwhile, the inrushing water was pouring aft into the engine room, which in prototype X-3 also housed the batteries. After flooding the diesel engine, this salt water reached the batteries and mixed with the battery acids. A suffocating chlorine gas was thus generated, and as it began to fill and contaminate the control room, two things happened almost simultaneously: they hit the bottom of Loch Striven and the lights went out.

They were stuck stern downward in the mud in 120 feet of water. This meant that the pressure of about five atmospheres was being exerted on the outside of the craft, and that the air inside, under compression by the inrushing water, would have to equal the pressure on the outside before they could open the hatch and escape. Had there been no chlorine gas, they could have breathed normally until the water rose to their mouths, but in order to live until the pressure equalized and they could escape, they would have to use their emergency equipment without delay.

"We'll put on our oxygen sets now, men," Lorimer said.

Called "Davis Submarine Escape Apparatus," this emergency equipment covered the face like a mask and had tubes leading to a gauge and distributor for controlling the flow and pressure of oxygen from its container. Down by the waist there was another attachment that would be used later if all went well and they escaped. It looked like an ordinary apron, and as a man climbed out through the hatch, he was to hold it out horizontally, like a parachute in reverse, to slow down his ascent to the surface and thus prevent too rapid a change of pressure on his body.

Once all three sets were on and functioning, Lorimer opened the sea cocks to increase both the inflow of water and the build-up of internal pressure. Though he did not share the thought with the two men under him, he knew that "when under water there is a tremendous tendency to panic, and the more you panic, the more oxygen you use."

Luckily, there was an extra oxygen set, so that if one man used up his supply too fast, there would still be a chance for them. If they all used up their oxygen too fast, two of them would perish.

"Breathe easily and naturally," he said, in the pitch darkness. "I've already unscrewed the hatch cover, so we'll be able to open it and get out just as soon as the pressure equalizes. That'll be in about forty minutes. Meanwhile, make sure your breathing apparatus is secure, and every five minutes I'll tap you on the shoulder to remind you to adjust the pressure. When I do, increase it by another pound."

Besides the awkward bow-up angle of the craft and the eerie sound of the water seeping in, the men had to contend with the chlorine gas burning their eyes, the sickening knowledge of its greenish-yellow color, and the awful realization that the more their minds fastened upon the vision of the sun shining on the surface of the water above them, the faster their hearts would beat and the more oxygen they would use. It was pure oxygen, and they were inhaling it, not as athletes do today, for a thirty-second pickup after a grueling session on the field, but constantly, under ever-increasing pressure on their lungs and circulatory systems. It had what Lorimer called "alarming effects," for as it enlivened their blood, it increased their comprehension of the danger they were in, their desire to escape, and also, with every passing minute, their chances of dying of oxygen poisoning.

To make the grinding tension more bearable, Lorimer removed his mouthpiece and said: "You'll go first, Gay. Then you, Laites. I'll follow. And don't forget, when you pass out through the hatch, hold your apron out in front of you. If you don't, you may break an eardrum or get a nasty dose of nitrogen in your blood."

Every five minutes, by the luminous hands of his waterproof watch, he reminded them to regulate their distributors. The wait seemed interminable, as the water, entering silently now, rose higher and higher around them, increasing with every inch the pressure against their bodies. It was not until the craft was about eighty per cent flooded that the water stopped rising, which meant that the compressed air was preventing any more from flowing in. The pressure inside and outside the craft had at last equalized.

"Gay," Lorimer said quietly, "try the hatch cover."

Gay pushed through the neck-high water, which in the darkness of the craft responded with strange, swampy sounds, and after several attempts that burned most of his remaining oxygen was able to push the hatch open. Water pounded down upon him and rushed in foaming streams toward every last cranny of unoccupied space in the craft. With a quick and final glance back into the compartment, he plunged upward and out as the remaining air, in a blizzard of bubbles, escaped with him.

In the midst of the disturbance caused by the water rushing in, Lorimer sensed that Laites was not making his way to the open hatch. Time seemed to stop when he found him in the darkness and realized that his oxygen had run out. He could feel him going limp in unconsciousness, and in the baleful stillness of the flooded craft he had what he later called a "miserable debate" with himself. Should he leave him here and escape before his oxygen ran out? Every second counted, and he was "scared stiff."

It was a special moment in John Lorimer's life, one that proved the validity of his own words: "If you are going to do anything dangerous, the best way to accomplish it is to train, train, train, so that in the excitement of the situation you do the thing automatically."

After quickly removing Laites's empty oxygen set, he replaced it with the extra set and started the flow of oxygen into his lungs. When even this did not bring him back to consciousness, Lorimer pushed him downhill through the water to the open hatch. There, grabbing him around both thighs, he lifted him, got his head through, and with all his strength pushed hard to give him as good a send-off as possible. Laites's oxygen set came off in the process, but at least he was on his way up to fresh air.

Lorimer, his own oxygen just about gone now from the exertion, then climbed out himself into the free-running waters of Loch Striven. "I only had one 'guff' of oxygen left in my bottle," he said, "and was practically unconscious when I managed to escape." But again he acted "automatically," and held out his apron to retard his ascent.

"I was never happier to see the sun," he said, "to say nothing of Don Cameron, who hauled me into a dinghy and told me that Gay and Laites were all right."

Cameron was there waiting for him because *Present Help*, the attending trawler, had seen signs of trouble and sent an emergency signal that brought helmet divers, salvage vessels, and every midget-submarine volunteer to the scene. In ten hours, X-3 was raised and on her way by rail to Portsmouth to be refitted and repaired.

During the next week, following thorough medical examinations of the three men trapped in the craft, Gay and Laites were granted transfers to another branch of the service. John Lorimer remained.

4

The decision to attack the *Tirpitz* in her protected anchorage in Kaafjord presented the British Admiralty with four major problems. The first—the choice of weapon to be used—was solved in May 1942 when successful trials of prototype X-3 were completed and construction began on six X-craft of a new and improved design.

The second problem—how to transport the six X-craft to within striking distance of their target—remained unsolved as late as February 1943, after various methods had been tried and rejected. The Admiralty knew that because their stronger fleet commanded the sea, the midgets could be safely carried by a surface ship and launched under cover of darkness, or just over the horizon, off the Norwegian coast. But secrecy was the guiding principle behind the entire mission, and there was little doubt that either a German submarine or a Luftwaffe reconnaissance plane would report the presence of a transport ship and her naval escorts off the Norwegian coast. Even if the midgets were concealed below deck until the moment they were lifted by derrick and lowered into the sea, the mere presence of a British flotilla off Norway would alert the Germans and make them warier than they already were.

Another possible method, that of sending the midgets across the North Sea under their own power, would have retained the necessary secrecy but added enormously to the already serious mechanical, navigational, and human risks involved. With the midgets traveling at six knots on the surface at night, and at about two knots submerged during the day, the 1,200-mile-journey from Scotland to the target area (assuming there were no rough seas to contend with) would take almost two weeks. After being confined that long in an iron box, sleeping only in snatches and in the most awkward positions, the men would be utterly exhausted, if not hopelessly seasick. Even if all six midgets made the crossing without developing mechanical trouble (a highly unlikely possibility), the men would be unfit physically, emotionally, and mentally to carry out the mission.

This method, too, was therefore rejected, and while others were being devised and discussed, the third major problem—how to obtain accurate information about the target area—was being worked on under equal pressure. The preliminary staff work, requiring hundreds of man-hours of time, was enormously complicated. The Admiralty's hydrographic department, using the data accumulated in prewar days, when the Royal Navy charted the waters of the world, prepared special charts of the entire Norwegian fjord area in the north. The Norwegian Navy was consulted to see if additional information could be supplied that would be of help. Fishermen who had escaped from German-occupied Norway in their herring boats and trawlers were asked for details regarding tides, currents, and depths in the passages leading into Altafjord and Kaafjord. All this varied information had to be considered in its direct bearing on the nature of the proposed attack, which was to be made with vessels whose potentialities were still largely a matter of guesswork.

But to make the charts both accurate and complete, the Admiralty needed up-to-date reconnaissance of the target area. Aerial photographs of the net defenses, the detection devices, the anchorage, and the disposition of the *Tirpitz* and her sister ships were absolutely essential to the success of the mission. There was no disagreement on this point, but Kaafjord was outside the range of Britain-based reconnaissance aircraft. They could reach Kaafjord from Scotland, but without refueling they could not return.

The solution to this problem came unexpectedly when, after

prolonged and trying negotiations with the Russians, an agreement was reached whereby the necessary British air crews and photographers would be sent by destroyer to Russia's year-round ice-free port, Murmansk. From there they would travel by jeep to Vaenga, where the Russians had cut a lane through a forest and constructed an airstrip. Makeshift hangars, built of freshly cut timbers, were concealed among the trees on either side. After setting up a film-developing laboratory for the preliminary reconnaissance runs, the pilots and photographers were to run a shuttle service, with Mosquito aircraft flown in by the RAF, between Vaenga and Scotland. For the last-minute sorties before the X-craft attack, the faster but shorter-ranged Spitfire was to be used, and the films were to be flown back to England by Catalina.

The fourth problem was that of establishing an espionage communications system between British Intelligence and Allied agents in Norway. Although many Norwegians had escaped from the *Tirpitz*-occupied part of Norway in the north, most had taken the mountain route into Sweden, where by law they were segregated and detained as aliens. Some accepted this internment willingly in anticipation of the war's end, but others eventually escaped and succeeded in reaching England. They came, however, with out-of-date information to pass on to the British.

Besides aerial photographs of the enemy's defenses, the Admiralty required firsthand information from men living and working in the Kaafjord area, men who saw the *Tirpitz* in her anchorage every day and had dealings with her officers and crew. Accurate and reliable reports were needed on the changing of the net patrols, the coming and going of supply ships to the side of the *Tirpitz,* her schedule for gunnery practice and the dismantling and cleaning of her guns and sonar equipment, the habits and idiosyncrasies of her officers and crew, their trips to the nearby town of Alta, and how their loneliness, boredom, and inactivity in the frozen north affected their vigilance over a ship they all believed invincible anyway. This vital information had to be gathered, collated, and kept up to date by daily intelligence messages from members of the Norwegian Resistance.

Although the great majority of Norwegians would have gladly taken some positive action against the Germans, only the most determined and resourceful were accepted as members of the Resistance. Among them was a lean, blond, wiry man named Torstein Raaby, who showed the same kind of courage, stamina, and spirit throughout the German occupation of his country as he did after the war, in 1947, when he joined the crew of *Kon Tiki* and took part in one of the most exciting and momentous voyages in the history of the sea.

Raaby had spent the year 1941 on a deserted, glacier-streaked island in the Arctic, an island important only for its meteorological station, which he operated and used as a cover for sending coded "weather reports" on Luftwaffe reconnaissance flights and German submarine operations to the Admiralty in London. In 1942, he and another agent, Alfred Henningsen, now a member of the Norwegian Parliament, operated a secret radio station in Tromsö, sending information to England about German defense and alarm systems.

The next year, when they were warned by a former Nazi that the Gestapo was on their trail, they crossed the mountains on skis and managed to reach Stockholm. From there, Raaby made his way by plane to England in March. He wanted a more active role in the war against the Nazis, and the British Admiralty offered him a dangerous one.

All along the Norwegian coast from Harstad to Hammerfest there were agents with secret radio transmitters, but now the most detailed information was needed about the *Tirpitz* and her supporting ships in their inland anchorage. Raaby's job would be to obtain this information from several men in the Kaafjord area and send in daily reports.

After four months of special training, he was given maps, ciphers, notes about trustworthy people, several false identity cards to enable him to travel where he wanted, eight special radio transmitter-receiver sets, nine hundred liters of gasoline, a gasoline engine, and 50,500 kroner. He was then taken by the Norwegian submarine *Ula* back to Norway, to a point just south of Trondheim, where the gasoline and gasoline engine and five of the eight radio sets were hidden in a cave for later use. The remaining sets, marked for the Kaafjord area, were packaged with a primer, detonator, and explosive, so that Raaby could instantaneously destroy them—and himself—in the event he was apprehended. It was a dreadful prospect, but Raaby knew that death was better than surrender to the torments of the Gestapo.

He was taken by another agent, Thorbjorn Johansen, to Tromsö, where he learned that his father had been taken by the Germans as a hostage. "If I have to crawl around Kaafjord on my hands and knees," he told Johansen, "I'll take my revenge on the *Tirpitz*."

With the help of another agent, Alfred Nilsen, he managed to make his way by herring trawler (the most common and innocuous-looking vessel to be found in the fjords of Norway) to Hammerfest, at the northern end of the German defense system. In the mountains around Hammerfest, he made contact with an old friend of his, Karl Rasmussen, who eyed the three special radio sets with the intense interest, Raaby later recalled, of "a born secret agent, which is what he was."

Their destination was the town of Alta, some fifteen miles away, a small arctic settlement that had knotted and secured itself at the crossings and along the diagonals of a network of hills. Houses built along these hills overlook a shopping district reminiscent of a nineteenth-century town in the American West, the Grand Hotel, and Alta Church, from whose tall and slender belfry Kaafjord can be clearly seen. It is a lovely town, set in its own little dell of solitude in a world usually composed of snow, a town where the elderly are pushed through snow-packed streets in chairs set on runners and the children ride to school on bicycles equipped with snow tires. Had it not been for its closeness to Kaafjord and the German naval squadron anchored there, it would have been quite out of touch with the war, and perhaps with the world as well. Unfortunately, it had its few incipient Quislings, though they were ostracized and despised by the majority, whose capacity for implacable loathing of the Germans far exceeded that of the British and the Americans.

Raaby and Rasmussen made the journey from Hammerfest as most people do in the north of Norway, by the waters of the fjords in a motor dinghy. When they arrived at Alta, they were met by Harry Pettersen, the third man chosen to work on the *Tirpitz* operation. Pettersen ran the town's taxi service; he also had a home along the edge of Kaafjord and made a practice of driving lower-echelon officers of the *Tirpitz* (the higher officers had their own cars) to and from Alta. He knew almost every one of the town's 5,000 inhabitants, whom he could trust and whom he should avoid, and, like everyone else in the Resistance, he was an expert at listening to both valuable information and the most useless chatter with the same patience and cunning. Besides, in the north of Norway there was no traffic to interfere with automobile conversation; a taxi driver who knew how and when to listen could learn a great deal, especially from German officers whose desire to feel at home in an occupied country went hand in hand with their need to believe the natives did not hate them.

A man like Pettersen, born and reared in Alta, who knew the area as he did his own hand, every hut, woodshed, barn, and warehouse, was naturally adept at providing a temporary hiding place for Raaby's equipment. The next most urgent assignment was to make Raaby an accepted member of the community by getting him a job.

Rasmussen worked in town with the Department of Roads, where he had a good friend in the person of the cashier's assistant. Most important, considering the stakes involved, the cashier's assistant was the kind of friend who would not have to be told, who in fact would not want to be told, the details or purpose of Raaby's mission. If what Rasmussen wanted him to do was anti-German, he would do it. So Rasmussen, after assuring him that there would be no loss of income (Raaby had been given enough kroner in London for just such a purpose), asked him to get sick. The man had bronchitis anyway, a condition serious enough to enable his doctor, another trusted friend of

Rasmussen's, to advise him to leave his job at least temporarily. Within a few days, he was replaced by a man whose papers were in perfect order, a man who indeed had several sets of papers, all of them in perfect order—Torstein Raaby.

Operating on the first principle of any agent, Rasmussen had told Raaby and the cashier's assistant only what each needed to know. The two men did not have to meet, so he saw to it that they never did; one did not have to know the other's name, so he never mentioned one's name to the other. Though he trusted them both completely, he did not want to burden them with secrets the Gestapo might some day force them to share. Nor did he want to be burdened with Raaby's secrets, haunted as he was by the thought of leaving a traceable series of links that might jeopardize the lives of other agents. The more gaps there were in what he knew about the Resistance, the less help he would be to the Gestapo if he were captured and broke down under torture.

Less than a week after Raaby started to work, the British Admiralty began receiving daily detailed reports about procedures and activities aboard the *Tirpitz*. Information came from Kaafjord fishermen, from Jan Johassen, the chief machinist on the boat that supplied the *Tirpitz* with provisions, and from Norwegian women hired by the Germans to clean the antiaircraft guns in the hills or do galley work aboard the ship. They listened to the German soldiers and sailors talking about gunnery practice, alertness drills, and the dismantling and cleaning of the ship's equipment. And they read the bulletin board every day. All this information was gathered by Rasmussen and Pettersen and given to Torstein Raaby, whose transmitter was hidden in his office in one of the Department of Roads buildings, where the Germans outnumbered the Norwegians ten to one. He sent his reports at night, by connecting his secret transmitter to a receiving aerial put up by a German officer who lived next door. "He was from the Todt organization," Raaby said. "I often talked with him, an agreeable fellow."

This impertinence added to Raaby's many dangerous delights in working against the Germans in Norway. They had taken his father as hostage, and here he was using one of their own aerials to send messages to the British. He was in contact with London every day with information about the *Tirpitz,* the *Scharnhorst,* and the *Lutzow,* and every day, without fail, the British Admiralty man at the other end would sign off with the words "Thank you very much!" Raaby even began sending information about troop movements, but he was told by London to concentrate on the German battleships—the *Tirpitz* in particular, that thorn in Churchill's side.

The Challenge Met

5

The six improved operational X-craft, or "ugly ducklings," as they were affectionately called, began arriving from Vickers Armstrong Limited in January 1943. Except for their numbers (X-5 through X-10), they were identical—unshapely lumps of metal looking more like water boilers than vessels capable of traveling beneath the sea.

Only forty-eight feet long, and weighing only thirty-nine tons fully stored and loaded, they had a maximum diameter of five and a half feet except under the periscope, where it was just possible for a small man to stand upright. Everywhere else it was necessary to crouch, sit, squat, or crawl. In fact, the question from the start for the engineers had been: How much space does a man need? To fit all the necessary equipment inside the hull and still leave room for a crew of four was a problem not only in engineering, but in human endurance, adaptation, and psychology as well.

Since most standard submarine equipment would not even fit inside the hull, these engineers had had to improvise with whatever comparable equipment was already under production or on the British market. To propel the X-craft beneath the surface, for example, they used an ordinary fan motor run by batteries. To propel her on the surface they used a London bus engine—the same four-cylinder, forty-horsepower diesel engine that at the height of the London blitz had made the old double-deckers so reliable. In short, they solved the problem, but not by much, and not without forgoing a human need here, a human comfort there.

As a result, climbing inside a midget was like climbing inside a clock. Wheels, levers, motors, gauges, pipes, cables, and valves protruded everywhere. There were overhead hatches and viewing ports to knock against, tanks and lockers to trip over, and odd spaces between machinery just large enough to trap or pinch a foot, finger, knee, or elbow. Indeed, since the propeller, rudder, and hydroplanes were included in the craft's over-all length, the actual internal space was closer to thirty-five feet. This "living" space, besides being jammed with machinery, compasses, pumps, tanks, and all the connecting pipes and cables, was divided into four compartments, only one of which was large enough to contain the entire crew of four men at one time.

The first, or forward, compartment contained the main battery, whose power, as in all submarines, lighted the ship, drove her pumps and auxiliary machinery, and propelled her when she was submerged. Wooden slats covered it, and when a man was off watch, he could crawl in on top of it, push the diver's equipment to one side, coil his legs around the food locker, and perhaps catch an hour or two of sleep.

The second compartment, or wet-and-dry chamber, which also contained the head, was designed to allow one member of the crew, the diver, to leave and re-enter the submarine while it was submerged, for the purpose of cutting antisubmarine nets at the entrance to enemy harbors.

The third compartment was the control room, and it was here, in extremely close company, that the crew operated all the complicated machinery, cooked, ate, and also tried to sleep. At the forward end sat the helmsman, surrounded by the wheels and levers that steered the craft and controlled its main ballast-tank-blowing system. Just aft of this steering seat came a slightly raised dome, where there was a wide-field bifocal night periscope, which was also used when the craft was submerged under a target and for sighting hostile aircraft. Next to it was the attack periscope, as slender as a walking stick, virtually invisible to the keenest submarine lookout, and yet beautifully clear. It could be raised telescopically nine feet, but the captain needed only two inches of it above the water to get an excellent view of what was going on around him.

There was, of course, no room for a galley, so a carpenter's gluepot in the control room served as a double boiler; an electric kettle provided hot water for cocoa or tea. Attempts were nevertheless made to cook meals from the contents of tins from the food locker. A can of stew or soup was quick and took little effort, but for a change, especially during an extended training exercise, a tin of corned beef mixed with a can of beans and a little water and then brought to a boil and topped with an egg did much to make the next can of stew more palatable. The desire to cook "something different" with such limited supplies and equipment tested the men's capacity for adaptation. They were there to learn how to endure in extremely cramped quarters, and improvising with food was part of the learning process.

The volunteers, in fact, made up what amounted to a private navy; they lived without privacy, secrets, or the usual formality of rank, but they lived also with dedication to the task at hand, and whether consciously or unconsciously, whether awake or asleep, whether working or eating, they listened.

"It's incredibly peaceful below the surface," said John Lorimer, who became second-in-command of X-6 under Donald Cameron. "Your hearing becomes very sensitive. Your life is spent listening, and after a time you hear the slightest noises. You're completely dependent upon noise, any noise, so that after awhile everything becomes accentuated. 'What's that?' you ask yourself whenever you hear something odd or different. 'Is it something that shouldn't be there?' Once, we were going along a hundred feet down and I heard this 'put-put.' What the hell's that? I wondered. We surfaced, and there they were, these porpoises escorting us, one after the other coming up to scrape against our bow. Great big playthings. It got so that when I came ashore, I found myself aware of things happening a long way off. In a restaurant I could hear conversations at other tables in a way I never could before."

The fourth compartment, right aft of the control room, contained the main motor and the London bus engine, which symbolized perhaps more than any other piece of equipment the wartime ability of the British to make do and "get on with it." The X-craft's performance in the operational area hinged upon this diesel engine, which had proved itself reliable under the most trying tests and trials. Normally used when the craft was on the surface, it sucked air down an induction trunk, which also served, rather inefficiently, as a voice pipe for the captain, who in rough weather lashed himself to it as a precaution against being washed off the casing into the sea.

In emergencies, when both speed and secrecy were essential, it was possible to use this same diesel engine while the craft was submerged to periscope depth. The induction trunk was then used as a snorkel, or twin air intake and exhaust, for the engine, but since neither a head valve nor a remotely operated hull valve was provided, snorkeling was a chancy undertaking that could end in the craft's becoming flooded within minutes. Most X-craft men preferred to trim their craft down to where its casing was nearly level with the water. The captain could then lie along the casing and offer only a very small radar or visual target.

The midget was nevertheless a versatile and powerful submersible—a complete submarine in miniature, with a steering and diving control no larger than the wheel of a child's car, a finger-sized periscope, and an escape hatch considerably smaller than a manhole. She cost little and carried a crew of only four, but she could do just about everything a submarine twenty times her size could do. Battery endurance was similar to that of larger submarines, but the available speeds were lower—cruising speed beneath the surface was about two knots, and top speed about six. Diving depth was nearly as good, even though X-craft, unlike larger submarines, had glass viewing ports above and at each side of the captain's command position in the control room. External steel shutters could be drawn across these viewing ports, from inside the craft, during deep dives or in the event of a depth-charge attack.

There were, however, basic differences in armament and range between the midget and a standard submarine. The midget carried no torpedoes, deck guns, rockets, or any other kind of projectile. A torpedo leaves a visible wake and explodes immediately on contact. This is no drawback in the open ocean, where a submarine holds the initiative by selecting the time, place, and conditions for its attack, but in a pond-sized body of water like Kaafjord, the entire German naval squadron would be alerted by the first explosion. All six midgets would be trapped and destroyed by depth charges.

The midget submarine was designed to act as a silent saboteur, without attracting attention or even suspicion, so instead of torpedoes, she carried two two-ton explosive charges. And instead of carrying them inside her hull, she carried them outside, one on the port side and one on the starboard. Each of these "side charges," as they were called, was crescent-shaped, so as to fit the outer contour of the hull from bow to stern, and each was equipped with watertight buoyancy chambers to make it neutrally buoyant under water. Its weight, that is, was the same as the weight of the water it displaced; it neither added to nor subtracted from the weight of the submarine. But when a side charge was released (by turning what looked like an ordinary steering wheel inside the X-craft), a copper strip between the hull and the charge peeled off, unsealing the buoyancy chambers and allowing enough water to enter to make the charge negatively buoyant, or heavier than water.

Another feature of the side charge was its timing device, which was also controlled from inside the craft. The delay was simply dialed, much as one sets an alarm clock to go off in two, three, or six hours, and the charge was released by turning the release wheel. Since the charge became negatively buoyant from the moment it was released, there was no danger of its shifting its position once it sank to the bottom. If placed under the keel of the *Tirpitz* in Kaafjord, for example, it would remain there until the timing device triggered the primer, which in turn would ignite the explosive charge.

The second basic difference between the midget and a standard submarine was in range. The midget had a range of only a few hundred miles, which meant she would have to depend on power not her own to negotiate the 1,200 miles of open sea from Scotland to the target area. At the same time, and at all costs, she would have to avoid detection by German submarines and reconnaissance planes based in Norway. This was the twofold problem that the Admiralty had been working on in vain for almost a year. It required a daring solution, one that perhaps only a great naval power like Britain would have felt challenged to find, let alone put into effect.

Finally, after months of exhaustive testing and experimentation, a scheme was devised whereby each midget would be towed to the target area—towed not by a ship, but by a full-sized submarine, and towed not on the surface, but submerged. Never before in the history of the sea had such a vast and complicated underwater towing operation been conceived, much less attempted. But once the Admiralty gave the scheme its approval, constructive suggestions began filtering in from both the engineers and the volunteers involved.

It was decided, for example, that each midget would have two crews, one for the operation itself and one for the passage. The operational crew would rest in the more comfortable, full-sized submarine during the towing operation, while the passage crew, in the midget at the end of the towline, would tend to all the electrical circuits and machinery. Every six hours the midget would surface to "guff through," change the stale air by raising the induction trunk and running the diesel engine for fifteen minutes—or longer if the battery and air bottles had to be recharged. For the remaining twenty-three hours of every day, she would remain submerged about forty feet deeper than her "parent."

The passage was to be made in four stages. In the first, on leaving Scotland, both parent and midget would travel very slowly on the surface until they reached the open sea. During the second stage, the parent would travel on the surface at approximately ten knots and the midget beneath the surface at a depth of from forty to fifty feet. The third stage would start two days before they came within sight of the Norwegian coast. From that point on, in order to avoid being spotted by enemy submarines and planes, both parent and midget would travel submerged except for the short periods when the midget —under the watchful eye of the submerged parent's periscope —surfaced to ventilate. The fourth and final stage would come at dusk just off the Norwegian coast, when both parent and midget would surface for the change-over of crews. The midget would then slip her tow and be on her own until the mission was completed and she returned to rendezvous with her parent submarine. Then once again the passage and operational crews would exchange places, for the homeward towing operation.

The rendezvous was to take place at night, and both the parent submarine and her midget had special infrared lights with which to signal each other. These lights were visible only through special goggles the Admiralty had devised, so that the rendezvous could not possibly be jeopardized by some lookout on a surfaced German U-boat.

But however carefully the engineers designed the X-craft, however strong, maneuverable, and undetectable they made her, she would still be only as reliable as the crew manning her, and it was upon this human element that the whole success of the operation depended. Underwater work at any time requires the highest qualities of courage and self-control, but when that work entails penetrating an enemy's innermost defenses, technical knowledge and efficiency, not to mention self-sacrifice, intelligence, and dedication, are needed in at least equal measure.

With all these qualities, though, the men had to have supreme confidence in their equipment and the most exact and intimate knowledge of its component parts. It was for this reason that when the hull of a midget had been completed and work was to start on installing the equipment, the crewmen chosen to man her were sent to the Vickers Armstrong yards to observe the operation. In this way they saw their vessel put together almost from scratch, they became familiar with her many parts, and, perhaps most important, they were able to have small adjustments made and refinements added to fit their particular taste and requirements. There was of course a limit to what they could suggest, but nobody minded if an extra food locker was added or a wheel shifted an inch or two this way or that.

After the mission had been given the code name "Operation Source" and classified "most secret," the six midgets and their crews were sent to Loch Cairnbawn, another sea loch in the far northwest of Scotland, where the mists and the moors aided the increasingly strict security measures being imposed. The crew of X-6 now consisted of Don Cameron, as commanding officer; John Lorimer, first lieutenant; Edmund Goddard, engine room artificer, and Richard Kendall, diver. For the next several weeks they lived, with the five other crews, in a manor house near the loch under conditions closely resembling those of the midgets they were to man. The damp manor house was allowed to remain that way. Each crew's sleeping quarters were cramped. The food was concentrated.

At sea there were endurance and adaptation trials to prepare the men for intense physical strain that would last for days. During the actual mission, they would be locked within arm's reach of one another in what amounted to a steel prison, unable to lie down fully or stand up, to wash or stretch their limbs, to eat or drink except from ration tins. Claustrophobia, cramps, psychic fears, and just plain wretchedness would have to be withstood while the most accurate maneuvers were accomplished and the greatest dangers overcome.

Since the shortage of space precluded an efficient air-conditioning apparatus, they would be breathing stale, humid air except during the few hours at night when they surfaced to charge their batteries. Condensation trickling down the inside of the pressure hull would have to be wiped up hour after hour, to prevent short circuits and, possibly, electrical fires. But the more they did this, the more they would sweat and the harder they would breathe, so that in the end their own bodies would be creating the very moisture they would be trying to combat. Unforeseen defects and difficulties were likely to pop up and have to be fixed in enemy waters when the tension was greatest. On such an "impossible" mission, anything could happen, and probably would, and it was for this "anything" that the men wanted to be prepared.

The captain was the navigator, strategist, and technician, and he alone gave orders. Though only a few years older than the young men under him, he had to have their complete trust and confidence and the steel nerves and inner strength to make hard decisions under fire. From his action station at the periscope in the center of the control room (where he could touch each of the others without taking a step in any direction), he learned how to conn his craft through narrow channels, across conflicting currents, and around buoy moorings and other obstacles.

Since no space was made available for an adequate chart table, he had to fold his chart to the area being plotted, much as one would a road map in a Volkswagen. But the chart soon became so wet from condensation that he came to depend on other aids to navigation—the stopwatch, the carefully timed shaft revolutions, and the gyro. In time he learned to use these to the point where, when close to a target, he could estimate his position accurately without recourse to manual plotting.

The diver had to learn how to climb out of the wet-and-dry chamber into the sea and return again. He had to know how to cut through every kind of antitorpedo net, and be able to stay under water for as much as six hours at a time. If his rubber suit developed a leak during a training exercise, he did not return to the craft and have it fixed, for he neither thought nor was allowed to think that training "didn't count." On the contrary, if his suit developed a leak, he worked in soaked underwear for six hours, just as he would if a leak developed during the mission itself.

The engine room artificer, who also acted as helmsman, was the trouble shooter of the four-man crew, a mechanical magician and contortionist combined, who not only had to know how to fix everything in the craft, but also how to reach what had to be fixed. To work on the engine, he had to crawl aft through a hatchway roughly two feet in diameter, lie flat on a foot-wide fuel tank, and reach in with tools where there was a clearance of only three or four inches. But it was not only in the engine room that things went wrong. In the control room itself the periscope might flood and have to be taken apart, dried, fixed, and put together again. A fan belt might snap, the trim motor might blow a fuse, a pump line might spring a leak. Since metal, volts, and moisture do not mix, and the X-craft was a combination of all three, breakdowns became as routine as the artificer's ability to fix them.

But the connoisseur of the X-craft, the first fiddler, so to speak, without whose finesse and expertise it could not have performed at all, was the first lieutenant, who sat at the after end of the control room before an array of gauges, wheels, and levers that controlled the depth, speed, and trim of the craft as well as its main motors and air compressor. He had to learn how to work these controls while the craft was running at different depths, different speeds, and in different densities of water, and while things were going on inside for which he had to compensate. A small toolbox passed from aft to forward could cause a bow-down angle if he did not make up for the change in the distribution of weight by adjusting a wheel here, a lever there.

As training progressed (and each crew trained only in the craft to which it was permanently assigned), the craft became an extension of the first lieutenant's arms, eyes, and mind. Like the old Model T Ford, each X-craft had its own crotchety personality and responded only to the manipulations of one esthetically as well as technically versed in its faults and capabilities.

John Lorimer knew that because of the dangers implicit in underwater work, many more men were being trained for the operation than would be able to take part. All the higher officers in charge—Captain W. E. Banks, D.S.C., R.N., Captain P. Q. Roberts, R.N., and Commander D. C. Ingram, D.S.C., R.N.

—had their eyes and ears open not only during actual training exercises but also in the wardroom in the evening, where a chance remark might say more about a man's fitness for the job than the man himself realized.

Lorimer had volunteered, at the age of nineteen, because the words "special and hazardous duty" had suggested "a bit of excitement." Now a year and a half older, he had experienced more than a bit of excitement; he had, in fact, almost lost his life. But X-6 was a part of him now; there was no turning back and no desire to. He was more determined than ever to be one of the twenty-four men chosen to take part in the mission.

6

It was the Admiralty's plan to attack the *Tirpitz* in the spring of 1943, before the hours of arctic darkness dwindled to the point where, for ten weeks in summer, there would be no darkness at all. The X-craft needed darkness for their secret passage up the fjords to the target area; they also needed a certain amount of moonlight to identify landmarks and make use of their carefully drafted maps and charts. The latest date for the attack was therefore considered to be March 9, 1943, when there would be a sufficient sliver of first-quarter moon and the necessary hours of darkness for the X-craft to make their approach unseen. After that date there would be either too much moon or, if they waited for it to wane in the last quarter, too few hours of arctic darkness.

Unfortunately, the decision to have regular full-sized submarines tow the six X-craft submerged to the target area was made only a month before the March 9 target date. This precluded a thorough training of the passage crews, upon whose stamina, dedication, and familiarity with the X-craft the success of the entire towing operation depended. Nor did it allow enough time to conduct towing trials at sea, test various towing ropes, determine the best towing depth, and perfect, under combat conditions, the change-over of passage and operational crews between the X-craft and their parent submarines.

Besides, according to Admiral Barry, "there were teething problems in the craft themselves—troubles which were to be expected in a new design of weapon but which it had optimistically been hoped would not occur. . . ."

Reluctantly, Barry informed the Vice Chief of Naval Staff that the operation would have to be postponed until the autumn, when conditions in the Arctic would be similar to those in March. The ten weeks of constant daylight would by then have ended, and the short, slowly lengthening nights would have begun. The only trouble with this new target date was that with each passing autumn day, as the arctic nights grew longer, the danger of snow squalls and blizzards increased. It was therefore decided to carry out the attack at the earliest date the hours of darkness allowed, so that the operation could be completed before weather conditions deteriorated. The period between September 20 and 25 was selected because the moon then would be in the last quarter, and the nights about five hours long. Both conditions met the requirements of the mission, so D day, the day the X-craft were to be slipped from their towing submarines to proceed up the fjords to the target area, was fixed for the twentieth of September.

"The time gained proved invaluable . . ." Admiral Barry said. "It insured that both the crews and the craft were trained and perfected to that concert pitch so vital to such an operation."

On September 1, 1943, security measures at Loch Cairnbawn, already strict, became severe. All leave was canceled, all correspondence forbidden, and every ship present in port retained until the completion of the operation. The men could of course write letters, but the letters would not be posted until after they sailed. No one was allowed to enter the base, much less leave it to visit a pub, where the slightest indiscretion could start a chain reaction of gossip, excitement, and rumor.

The next day and the day after, the six towing submarines, —*Thrasher, Truculent, Stubborn, Syrtis, Sceptre,* and *Sea Nymph,* all of them fitted with special towing equipment that had been devised during towing trials—slid into the waters of Loch Cairnbawn. They came quietly, one at a time at three-hour intervals, and by late afternoon of the second day, with the setting sun behind their lofty conning towers, they looked like giant shadows of themselves—black, elongated, faceless, unknown. By their size alone they made the X-craft, lying so low in the water that every boat's wake washed over their casings, look more like floats devised by children than weapons to be used against a battleship a thousand times their size.

Don Cameron, whose son, Iain, was only four months old, made a will and arranged matters with the paymaster in the event the mission ended in disaster. He felt "somewhat sheepish" about the will, he later told his wife, but thought it best to be "on the safe side." After eleven years at sea, he was too experienced, too thoughtful, and too old (twenty-seven) to think of himself as "immortal."

This tendency to look ahead and be prepared had also led to Cameron's acute awareness of the fact that several of the Manila towing lines had parted during towing trials, and that new, stronger lines had been ordered. The new lines, only two inches in diameter but made of nylon, were to be the same as those used for towing gliders in the air. They had only recently come into nautical use, and Cameron was set on getting one for his X-6 before the towing operation started. When he made this clear to the bosun of the *Bonaventure,* in the friendliest way possible, he happened to be in the process of stuffing his pipe with tobacco. It had always been a pacifying experience for the bosun to watch Cameron stuff his pipe, and this time was no exception. The pipe became an agreeably interested third party to the conversation, a kind of benign arbiter. Of course the bosun made no promises, but a few days later, when only three nylon towing lines arrived, Cameron, old salt that he was, got one of them. "The motto is," he later told his wife, "always keep in with the bosun."

Each X-craft had by now been assigned to a parent submarine, and the operational and passage crews of each had been named by Commander G. P. S. Davies. Since there would be no need for a diver in the X-craft during the towing operation, the passage crew, including the commanding officer, would consist of three men.

When the list appeared on *Bonaventure*'s bulletin board, it read as follows:

X-5, towed by *Thrasher* (Commanding officer Lt. A. R. Hezlet)

Passage:	Commanding officer	J. H. Terry-Lloyd
	Crew	B. W. Element
		N. Garrity
Operation:	Commanding officer	H. Henty-Creer
	Crew	T. J. Nelson
		D. J. Malcolm
		R. J. Mortiboys

X-6, towed by *Truculent* (Commanding officer R. L. Alexander)

Passage:	Commanding officer	A. Wilson
	Crew	J. J. McGregor
		W. Oxley
Operation:	Commanding officer	D. Cameron
	Crew	J. T. Lorimer
		R. H. Kendall
		E. Goddard

X-7, towed by *Stubborn* (Commanding officer A. A. Duff)

Passage:	Commanding officer	P. H. Philip
	Crew	J. Magennis
		F. Luck
Operation:	Commanding officer	B. C. G. Place
	Crew	L. B. C. Whittam
		R. Aitken
		W. M. Whitley

X-8, towed by *Sea Nymph* (Commanding officer J. P. H. Oakley)

Passage:	Commanding officer	J. Smart
	Crew	W. H. Pomeroy
		J. G. Robinson
Operation:	Commanding officer	B. M. McFarlane
	Crew	W. Y. Marsden
		R. X. Hindmarsh
		J. B. Murray

X-9, towed by *Syrtis* (Commanding officer M. H. Jupp)

Passage:	Commanding officer	E. A. Kearon
	Crew	A. H. Harte
		G. H. Hollis

Operation:	Commanding officer	T. L. Martin
	Crew	J. Brooks
		V. Coles
		M. Shean

X-10, towed by *Sceptre* (Commanding Officer I. S. McIntosh)

Passage:	Commanding officer	E. V. Page
	Crew	J. Fishleigh
		A. Brookes
Operation:	Commanding officer	K. R. Hudspeth
	Crew	B. Enzer
		G. G. Harding
		L. Tilley

On September 5, all six X-craft were hoisted on board *Bonaventure* for the fitting of the live side charges of highly explosive amatol. A certain amount of spot welding was necessary for this operation, and while the second charge was being fitted on X-6, under the watchful eye of First Lieutenant John Lorimer, a spark from a workman's torch started a fire among the ten other side charges lying on deck. The five or six workmen took one look, panicked, and fled to the forward part of the ship.

The twelve side charges, taken together, represented twenty-four tons of amatol, enough explosive power to destroy not only all six X-craft on deck, but also the *Bonaventure* and everyone aboard. If the concussion ignited the ship's fuel tanks, every ship in port would be endangered. Tons of hot metal, flaming debris, and burning oil would be thrown out over the confined waters of the loch. The windows of homes a mile away would be smashed as the flaming oil on the water spread to other ships and they, too, one after another, caught fire and exploded. The six parent submarines might escape the conflagration by diving, but Operation Source would be dead and buried before it had begun.

Had Lorimer followed the workmen's example and fled, no one would have blamed him. But without a second's hesitation, he and another lieutenant on the afterdeck ran for hoses, poured gallons of water on the blaze, and quickly extinguished it.

When the workmen returned, rather sheepishly, to continue the job, Lorimer found himself a bit embarrassed, too, for, according to the explosives experts on board, there had been absolutely no danger. The amatol would merely have melted with the heat; it needed detonating to explode.

Meanwhile, although the Mosquito planes for the preliminary reconnaissance of the target area had been ready to leave England for Vaenga, Russia, as early as August 21, weather conditions had made it impossible to carry out this part of the plan. This hampered the daily briefings of the X-craft captains, and added to the suspense, for in order to keep to the strict schedule set for D day—the slipping of the midgets from their parents on September 20 off the Norwegian coast—Operation Source would have to sail from Loch Cairnbawn no later than September 11. Luckily, the three Spitfires to be used for the final reconnaissance arrived at Vaenga just in time, on September 3, exactly eight days before the towing operation was set to start.

Weather conditions kept them grounded for four days, until September 7, when the first sortie flown over the target area created another crisis. According to the pilot, only the pocket battleship *Lutzow* was in her berth in Kaafjord. This report confirmed a radio message received in London only a few hours earlier from Torstein Raaby in Alta. Raaby, Rasmussen, and Pettersen had seen the German warships leave Kaafjord under cover of darkness but were unable to supply any additional information. They had no way of knowing (any more than London did) that the *Tirpitz*, the *Scharnhorst*, and ten destroyer escorts were on their way north through the arctic mists to attack Spitsbergen. Nor was there any way of finding out, since two days later, on September 9, when the *Tirpitz* appeared off Spitsbergen and the island's wireless station attempted to inform the Allied wireless station in Iceland, the

Tirpitz jammed the message and then destroyed the wireless station itself.

The entire X-craft mission hinged upon the *Tirpitz* and her sister ships being in the fjords. Even if they moved from Kaafjord to the Narvik or Trondheim areas of Norway, as they had done before, the attack could still be carried out, because mission plans had already taken these two possibilities into account and made allowances for them. But until the Admiralty knew where the German warships were, or at least where they were headed, it would be both foolhardy and extravagant to launch Operation Source.

At Loch Cairnbawn, the X-craft captains studied and restudied charts and contour maps of all three possible target areas while awaiting final orders from Admiral Barry, who was himself waiting tensely in London for word from one of the Resistance agents operating radio transmitters along the Norwegian coast. Had German Intelligence, he wondered, learned of the impending X-craft attack and informed Admiral Oskar Kummetz in Kaafjord? Was the *Tirpitz* hurrying home to Germany, or on her way to some new secret anchorage in the north of Norway? At the Admiralty, the thought of Winston Churchill wondering, too, where the *Tirpitz* was only added to the tenseness of these hours of doubt and indecision.

The six X-craft had made their final dives with full operational equipment and crews; they had undergone final towing trials with their respective parent submarines and been stocked with provisions—concentrates mostly, and what Lorimer called "beautiful little tins of orange juice from California." Passage and operational crews were ready to leave. All they lacked was a destination.

Finally, on the tenth of September, Raaby reported the return of the *Tirpitz* and the *Scharnhorst* to Kaafjord. A few hours later, visual and photographic Spitfire reconnaissance not only confirmed this report, but also obtained full details of the disposition of the ships and their net defenses. When these details were signaled to London from Russia, late in the afternoon on September 10, Admiral Barry flew immediately by military aircraft to Loch Cairnbawn "to see the crews before they sailed and to witness the start of this great enterprise."

No actual photographs of the Spitfire reconnaissance were available for the final briefing, because the Catalina flying them from Russia had not arrived. It was frustrating to be without them (Barry wanted each captain to have a set to study during passage to the target area), but Operation Source had been full of frustration from the start. He was used to it, disregarded it, and invited all operational and passage captains to dine with him that evening aboard the *Titania,* the depot ship for the parent submarines.

"Any doubts which I might have entertained could not possibly survive the infectious confidence of these young men," he later observed. "This confidence was not in any way the outcome of youthful dare-devilry, but was based on a firm conviction that their submarines were capable of doing all their crews demanded, and the crews quite capable of surmounting any hazards which it was possible for human beings to conquer."

When the evening was over, and Cameron returned to *Bonaventure* for his last night's sleep in Loch Cairnbawn, he started his personal account of Operation Source, addressing it to his wife, Eve, whom he had nicknamed "Tubs."

"Darling, I am writing this for your enjoyment, I hope, and for Iain's when he is old enough to take an interest in such matters. Am putting in no dates in the earlier part of the narrative for obvious reasons, and our passage up [to the Arctic] will be fairly scanty in detail.

"Friday evening. Bidden to dine with Claude [Admiral Barry] on *Titania.* Eat, drink and be merry . . . Excellent dinner, sitting on Claude's left between him and Willie Banks. Usual shop. Very optimistic, perhaps a trifle over-optimistic. I'm of the opinion that it is already regarded as a 'walk over,' and I have a nasty suspicion of over confidence. Good thing, perhaps—canny Scot . . . My condition a trifle hazy on return to *Bonaventure!* Lovely clear night, moon almost full, good weather ahead, thank God. Scenes of merry making [among

X-craft crews] on my return. Turn in for my last night in a comfortable bunk. Good night, Tubs."

The next morning, when the Spitfire photographs still had not arrived, Barry signaled the Commander in Chief, Home Fleet, his intention to start the towing operation anyway, so that D day would fall on September 20 as planned. A detailed interpretation of the net defenses could be made when the photographs arrived, and the results signaled to the parent submarines before they reached their slipping positions off the Norwegian coast. He did not want to postpone the mission even for a day if he could possibly help it, owing to the waning moon. The precarious passage up the fjords to the target area had enough against it without adding total darkness.

And so the order was given. Operation Source, one of the most extraordinary missions of World War II, would start that day, in the afternoon at four o'clock.

The Passage

7

Saturday, September 11, 1600 hours

First away was X-6, towed by the submarine *Truculent*. It was a tense and thrilling moment, one that Don Cameron, John Lorimer, Edmund Goddard, and Richard Kendall, all of them perched atop *Truculent*'s conning tower, would never forget. Admiral Barry, excited himself, had come out in *Bonaventure*'s motorboat the better to move about on the water and see everything there was to see.

"We move off . . . down the loch past *Bonaventure, Titania* and the others," Cameron wrote his wife about the launching. "Whistles as we pass *Titania.* More whistles, and cheering and saluting as we pass *Bonaventure.* All hands out to give us a send-off. Wonder what they're thinking? 'No more trouble from those bastards for a few days, still, good luck to the sods.'

"Admiral Barry, Willie Banks and Captain Roberts await us at the entrance and wish us all the best. Whistles and saluting. Whistles and saluting. Round the point past Raven's Rock. Now it is up to us. . . .

"Feel slightly depressed because my little red cap has disappeared. Is it my Highland blood taking this as an omen? I still have Bungey, though, so all's well. [Bungey, a little wooden dog given to him by his wife, always lived in his trousers pocket.] Why should I, a product of modern civilization, be affected by such things? There appears to be no logic to it but there it is. I look at the familiar hills and islands and wonder when I shall see them again. Said a little prayer for us all, darling. . . ."

Truculent's captain, Lieutenant Robert Alexander, was a Scot like Cameron, a huge bear of a man, whose broad, imposing face was made even more so by the tufted sideburns running down his cheeks. He and Cameron stayed in the conning tower to see how the tow behaved when X-6 dived for the night.

"There she goes," he said as X-6 slid beneath the surface.

But to their surprise, she soon surfaced again. The periscope fairing was loose and banging and had to be either mended or removed. *Truculent* slowed down while Lieutenant Wilson, commanding officer of the passage crew of X-6, climbed out the hatch, investigated, and finally ripped the fairing off and ditched it.

When X-6 dived again, Cameron and Alexander waited a few more minutes, then went below for their first meal and first night's sleep at sea. Cameron, lent a bunk by the chief engineer for the passage, was by no means uncomfortable. Goddard slept with the crew, the tall Lorimer on the wardroom settee, and little Kendall, who amused everyone the first night by changing into pajamas, in a sling in the alleyway. They had all offered to take turns at watch-keeping duties, "to help pass the time and keep their hand in," and were at once accepted as part of the crew.

Following X-6 around Raven's Rock and on out to sea was the submarine *Syrtis,* towing X-9 with a Manila rope so heavy that two balsa-wood floats were attached to it at intervals to take up some of the weight. Next came *Thrasher,* towing X-5 with nylon; *Sea Nymph,* towing X-8 with Manila; *Stubborn,* towing X-7 with Manila; and, finally, *Sceptre,* towing X-10 with nylon.

So started a towing operation unparalleled in the annals of the sea, an operation as unique, and certainly as hazardous, as the mission that was to follow it. Each towing line was approximately two hundred yards long, and running through the center of each was a telephone cable that connected the towing submarine with the X-craft behind it. The delay in the delivery of all six nylon towropes was in fact due to this ingenious device: each rope had to be custom made. On the other hand, the mission could not be postponed any longer, and the Manila ropes originally chosen for the operation were already equipped with telephone cable.

Once out at sea, the six towing submarines traveled in roughly parallel lanes about ten miles apart, at an average speed of ten knots, with each X-craft, like a kite at the end of a string in a heavy wind, moving up and down through a hundred feet or more of water. It was a movement tending toward the worst kind of seasickness, and the passage crews—except for fifteen minutes every six hours, when they surfaced to change the stale air—had to endure it for hours and days. They could lessen it considerably by filling the ballast tank forward and running at a bow-down angle, but the stability thus gained was offset by the danger added. If the tow parted, the heavy towrope at the bow, plus the weight of the water in the ballast tank forward, could send the craft plunging headlong to the bottom.

In addition to seasickness, the three men in each X-craft had to endure appalling discomfort during passage. Dampness penetrated their clothing, wet their hair, and seemed to narrow the already cramped space they shared. Able to sleep only in snatches, they had to work constantly to keep the craft in condition for the operational crew. There were electrical insulations to be checked, motors to be tested, machinery to be greased and oiled, air bottles and batteries to be recharged, bilges to be dried, bulkheads and hull plates to be wiped of condensation, records to be written, readings to be made on all electrical circuits, and meals to be prepared.

This twenty-four-hour assignment had to be done in shifts, for while the craft was submerged, which was most of the time, one member of the crew had to give his complete, undivided attention to the depth gauge and inclinometer bubble. An up-and-down movement of the craft was normal, but too sudden a downward pitch could mean the tow had parted.

"Nothing is worse than to watch one dial, one gauge, for two hours," John McGregor, of X-6's passage crew, said. "You know that a sudden depth change, say from 100 to 130 feet in ten seconds, may mean the end, and you do your best to be attentive. But try it for two hours and you can't help it, you think of home, girls, your boyhood. . . ."

Time below in the midget soon ceased to have any meaning. The three men were supposed to rotate watches every two hours, so that there would always be two men on watch and one man off. But sometimes the two on watch, if only because they had padded seats and were relatively comfortable, remained on watch in something like a stupor for three, four, or even six hours. Off watch there was only the primitive sleeping pallet in the battery compartment forward, or the engine in the engine room aft to lean against, or the periscope in the control room to coil around. Real sleep was almost impossible anyway, since in time, in order to remain alert on watch, all three members of the crew were forced to take Benzedrine. When off watch, if they had no work left to do, they sometimes simply slipped their minds into neutral and waited for the time to pass. Mostly, though, they worked hard off watch, not only because there was almost always work to be done, but also because by exerting themselves they helped ward off the cold, almost tactile dampness, which increased the closer they got to the polar region.

The first four days at sea passed with only minor mishaps. Good weather enabled all six parent submarines to make good speed with their X-craft submerged in tow. Every two hours the passage crews communicated with their respective operational crews by telephone, and every six hours they surfaced for fifteen minutes, to change the stale air and recharge the batteries.

Wednesday, September 15

Early in the morning on this fifth day of the passage, an electrifying message was signaled by the British Admiralty to the submarines taking part in the operation. A detailed interpretation of the Spitfire photographs, which had arrived in London from Russia only a few hours after the X-craft had left Loch Cairnbawn, revealed the latest positions of the net defenses and the three target ships. The pocket battleship *Lutzow* was anchored in Langefjord, one of those fingerlike extensions of Altafjord. The *Scharnhorst* had returned to her position just inside the antisubmarine nets in Kaafjord, and, most important of all, the *Tirpitz,* having moved into her net cage at the far end of Kaafjord five days earlier, had not moved and showed no signs of moving.

This information led to the adoption of Target Plan Four, which allocated X-5, X-6, and X-7 to attack the *Tirpitz;* X-9 and X-10, the *Scharnhorst;* and X-8, the old, flush-decked *Lutzow.*

"We were all in top spirits," Cameron later recalled. "It was high time to get cracking."

That same day, though Cameron did not know it, his cautiousness about towlines was borne out by what happened in another lane of the operation. The submerged X-8 was being towed by her surfaced parent, *Sea Nymph,* at eight knots. Except for the total of one hour of surface ventilation every day, the passage crew of X-8, like the other crews, had been submerged for five days. The men were torn between weariness and the effects of Benzedrine, between wanting to sleep and being unable to.

Suddenly, like a blindfolded man making the utmost use of his other four senses, Jack Smart, X-8's commanding passage officer, got the feeling that his craft was free and drifting. Grabbing the phone (it was exactly four o'clock in the morning), he put the receiver to his ear and heard nothing, no static, no crackle, no buzz. X-8 had been allotted one of the three Manila towlines, and it had parted.

Within seconds he was emptying the main ballast tanks of

water. As the compressed air rushed in with its reassuring hiss, the depth-gauge needle stopped moving, then slowly swung back toward the lower numbers. When the craft surfaced, and Smart climbed out on the casing, he saw nothing around him but the open sea. How long had they been adrift? The gauzy light of dawn was spreading farther and farther over the water, but, despite visibility of at least five miles, there was no sign of *Sea Nymph*. After checking his position, which was 69° 04′ North, 08° 14′ East, he decided to follow along in the direction *Sea Nymph* had been traveling. That way, when *Sea Nymph* realized the tow had parted, she could backtrack along the same route and pick them up with the auxiliary tow.

As it happened, *Sea Nymph* did not realize until six o'clock that the tow had parted. X-8 was due to surface to ventilate at that time, and when she did not, the officer on watch, looking anxiously astern, informed his captain, Lieutenant J. P. H. Oakley, who at once had the tow checked and found it had parted. Six hours had passed since the previous surfacing, so X-8 might be anywhere from ten to fifty miles away. Oakley turned *Sea Nymph* back on her track to search, but by noon there was still no sign of the errant craft. The wind had increased to fifteen miles per hour, the sky was overcast, and the sea had become "rough to very rough." Oakley kept it to himself, but the thought occurred to him that, in order to be sighted, X-8 would have to remain on the surface, and that on the surface in this sea she would hop about like a cork. Was she heading home submerged under her own power, or was she already lost?

8

In the lane adjacent to *Sea Nymph*'s, X-7 was experiencing the full effects of the "rough to very rough" sea. Even though submerged, she was at the mercy of the tow, which responded with brutal accuracy to every movement of *Stubborn* on the surface. They were in a following sea, and every time the stern of *Stubborn* rose with the swell and then precipitously fell in the trough, X-7, two hundred yards behind and roughly forty feet below, was hauled from port to starboard and back again with the most upsetting corkscrew motion. The craft rolled and pitched, heeled over and rose, then suddenly, as *Stubborn*'s stern sank in a trough, plunged headlong in a power dive.

The men inside the tiny craft, retching from seasickness, were being thrown this way and that, against bulkheads and into one another. They could not just hold on until the sea above them calmed, for if they did, the ever-present beads of condensation would build up, trickle down behind the control board, and cause one short circuit after another. They had to clean up their own mess and keep to their schedule of duties despite the erratic jouncing of the craft.

Lieutenant Peter Philip, the commanding passage officer of X-7, was a short, stocky, hook-nosed man with great stamina and a natural enthusiasm that made him popular with everybody. When the X-craft men learned that before the war he had been known to thousands of South Africans as "Uncle Peter" on Capetown's "Children's Hour," he became Uncle Peter to them as well.

A member of South Africa's Naval Forces and one of the first to volunteer for X-craft duty, Philip had expected the passage to be bumpy, but nowhere near this staggering. In the tumultuous privacy of the tiny craft conditions were worse than he had ever known them, even on the surface. He could feel the swell of the sea above him even down at eighty feet, as *Stubborn*, moving forward in a series of swooping rushes, made a veritable whip of the tow. Philip expected it to part at any moment. He also had a vague suspicion that one, if not both, of the craft's side charges had been lost, or at least flooded. Then the telephone became inaudible; cups were knocked off shelves; the craft shook and quivered in one convulsive spasm after another.

Shortly after noon the telephone came alive again, and at 1213 *Stubborn* herself dived, telling Philip that a submarine, "believed to be a U-boat," had been sighted. Actually, it was the lost X-8, whose tiny hull had been mistaken for the half-submerged conning tower of a U-boat. It was an understandable mistake, because no one connected with the mission was supposed to be that close. The routes, although roughly parallel, were ten miles apart.

Both *Stubborn* and X-7 remained down for a little over an hour, until 1323, when they surfaced together, *Stubborn* to continue the tow, and X-7 to get a little fresh air. The "U-boat" had disappeared, so when X-7 dived again, *Stubborn* proceeded surfaced on course.

Godfrey Place, in *Stubborn*'s conning tower with her captain, Lieutenant A. A. Duff, had received no complaints from Philip in X-7, and this only stimulated his imagination of what was going on inside the craft. He, too, was concerned about the tow, and some two hours later, at 1550, when one of *Stubborn*'s lookouts let out a shout, he did not have to be told what had happened. The lookout had noticed a snapping movement in the water astern, and then, seconds later, had seen the end of the tow whipping back against the submarine's casing. This was another of the three Manila towlines used in the operation, and it, too, had parted.

In X-7's control room, though, Philip was not immediately aware of what had happened. He had given up his turn on the sleeping pallet in the battery room forward, partly because of the Benzedrine he had taken and partly because the real enemy, time, had to be fought no matter where you were. It was no doubt his sophisticated sense of hearing, the sense that submarine men, more than anyone else, associate with balance and equilibrium, that told him what had happened. The rub of water against the craft's casing had lessened; her bow had stopped fighting the pull; there was the unmistakable suggestion that she was drifting and turning at a lazy, bow-up angle.

It took Philip only seconds to send full pressure into the ballast tanks and bring the craft to the surface again. The sea was as heavy as ever, and the craft, with all headway lost, pitched and rolled at its mercy. The waves, washing over the casing, seemed almost to be waiting for Philip as he climbed out the hatch to see if *Stubborn* was still in sight. Pounding and crashing and throwing up spray, they sought his feet, legs, and even torso as he clambered to the induction trunk and held fast against the endless buffeting.

Suddenly, between two waves, he caught a glimpse of *Stubborn*. She was alerted to the tow's parting and was veering round to launch a dinghy and secure a new tow. In this sea it would be a risky operation, and Duff had all hands standing by. He maneuvered *Stubborn* to within seventy feet of X-7 and set up a lee calm for the dinghy, to which a light lead line had been made fast.

In the dinghy, with one end of the new tow, was huge and powerful Bob Aitken, the diver of X-7's operational crew. At his signal, the men aboard *Stubborn* began paying out on the lead line, allowing the wind and waves to carry him down toward X-7. He would not have been able to row in any case, for he was too busy with the tow, which had to be hauled down twelve-foot troughs and over heaves of sea through seventy feet of water. The men aboard *Stubborn* did not want to pay out either the lead line or the hawser too fast, for they knew that any slack would only add to the hawser's weight. Aitken had to haul the hawser himself, at the same speed as the sea was carrying him down to leeward, and then pass it to X-7. If he let go, he and the tow would have to be hauled back and the operation repeated.

Meanwhile, Philip, with the wind snatching at his clothes and pulling at his hair and taking his breath away, was creeping forward toward X-7's bow to meet him. They had trained for months in heavy seas off Scotland for just such a contingency, so no words were exchanged and no unnecessary movements made. Aitken, with about six feet of towline in the dinghy with him, was lucky with his first try at passing it to Philip, and Philip just as lucky at shackling it to X-7's bow. The operation was completed quickly, but in the roughly racing sea, the lead line from *Stubborn* to the dinghy parted. Aitken felt the snap in the way the dinghy reacted to it. He was in real trouble now and, holding on, threw a quick glance back over the gray scudding water toward *Stubborn*. How was he, in an inflated rubber boat as capricious in the water as an empty bottle, to get back?

It was one of those times of crisis when training and luck merge. As the featherweight dinghy bounded up on a heave of sea, Aitken saw the submerged towline in the water beneath him. He waited for the next trough and, like a man fishing with his hands, when it came grabbed hold of the line. The men aboard *Stubborn* could do nothing to help him, because the tow had been made secure to X-7 and could not be hauled in. He had to haul himself back, hand over hand, with his torso more in the sea than in the dinghy, and with his breath coming in gasps between nauseating gulps of salt water. The tow, depending upon the rise and fall of the water, was almost too submerged and slack or too taut and slippery. But he finally got to within reach of a heaving line from *Stubborn*, grabbed it, let go of the tow, and allowed himself to be hauled in the rest of the way. It was a splendid performance, and the men aboard *Stubborn*, stretching out their arms to reach him, pulled him aboard with a pawing, brutal fondness.

Aitken, pulling air into his lungs, but smiling, too, luxuriated for a moment in that wonderful mission-accomplished feeling. Surely nothing facing him in Kaafjord could take more out of him. But that was wishful thinking, and he knew it. In fact, he had more tension and sheer horror awaiting him in Kaafjord than any other man connected with the mission.

No sooner did the towing operation pick up again, with *Stubborn* on the surface and X-7 submerged, than Philip realized he had slipped the shackle pin into the shackle but had forgotten to screw it, which meant that the only thing holding it in place (if it *was* still in place) was the strain the tow was exerting on it. Surfacing as quickly as possible, he opened the hatch, climbed out, crept along the casing to the bow, and, with the head-on waves pounding into him, saw that the pin and the tow were still in place. It took great effort, using the tapered end of a spanner wrench as a lever, to turn the shackle pin against the strain of the tow, but he finally managed to screw it in all the way. When he climbed back down the hatch, he took advantage of the fresh air streaming through the craft to light a soggy cigarette. He was soaking wet, but he did not care. The water from his shoes and trousers was dripping harmlessly between the deck boards into the bilges; *Stubborn* was towing at a sluggish but peaceful five knots.

It was not until he had finished the cigarette and was preparing to dive again that he saw, through the periscope, "X . . . X . . ." ("Stand by for panic") flashes from *Stubborn*. Philip alerted his two-man crew and waited, but nothing happened. *Stubborn* remained on the surface; so he did, too. Then came even more puzzling flashes: "T . . . T . . ." What was *Stubborn* trying to tell him?

The mysterious flashes from *Stubborn* were in fact signals to X-8, the errant midget mistakenly identified earlier as the conning tower of a U-boat. X-8 had sighted *Stubborn* at 1630, while *Stubborn* was passing X-7 the second tow. Lieutenant Duff now knew that the suspected U-boat had been X-8, and after being told by X-8 what had happened, he made some quick calculations, based on information supplied by X-8 as to where and when it had happened and what course *Sea Nymph* had been steering at the time. Then, altering course, he proceeded at a slow speed, with X-7 in tow and X-8 just off his starboard beam, in search of *Sea Nymph*. The time was 1718.

Two hours later, at 1900, when dusk fell without *Sea Nymph* being sighted, Duff used his hearty voice through a megaphone to tell X-8 to proceed northward with him until daybreak, by which time he would have alerted *Sea Nymph* that her midget had been found.

"Steer 046 degrees," he shouted, to preclude any chance of their being separated in the darkness. He then reported the situation by wireless to Admiral Barry, in London, who in turn signaled *Sea Nymph* and fixed a rendezvous for the next day.

Unfortunately, Duff's big voice, even through a megaphone, proved unequal to the wind and spray between him and the bobbing midget off his starboard beam. X-8 had understood him to say "Steer 146 degrees," so that by midnight she had veered way off course and was no longer in sight. Even when Duff used his special infrared signal lights, visible only through the special goggles designed for the mission, he received no reply.

9

Thursday, September 16

At 0300, as dawn bloomed over the misty waters around *Stubborn,* Duff, using binoculars, screened the area around him in the hope of spotting X-8. Three hours had passed since he had tried in vain to signal her, but there was always the chance that she had had mechnical trouble and was trying to catch up. She was nowhere in sight, though. After telling the officer of the watch to keep a sharp lookout, he went below to get some rest.

Fifteen minutes later, the officer of the watch sighted a submarine off *Stubborn's* starboard quarter. Realizing at once that she was riding too high in the water to be X-8, he thought she might be a U-boat. Then, with great relief and excitement, he recognized all the identifying marks of a British submarine. She was *Sea Nymph,* on her way to the rendezvous with *Stubborn* and X-8 that the Admiralty in London had ordered hours earlier. The alerted Duff, back in the conning tower, at once passed on all the necessary information to *Sea Nymph,* who proceeded southward to look for her errant charge. *Stubborn* and X-7 continued northward toward their slipping positions off the Norwegian coast.

It was not until 1700, almost fourteen hours later, that *Sea Nymph* sighted and made contact with X-8, whose crew had been without sleep or rest for thirty-seven hours. Lieutenant Smart, his face strapped with fatigue and tension, his bloodshot eyes rimmed with grease, had hardly been off his feet in all that time. He was so exhausted after making the new tow fast that

Lieutenant B. M. McFarlane, commanding officer of the operational crew, insisted that the transfer of crews be carried out without delay. There was still some sea running, but not enough to make the change-over dangerous. After two uneventful trips with the dinghy, McFarlane, Marsden, Hindmarsh, and Murray took over from Smart, Pomeroy, and Robinson.

The longer the towing operation lasted, the more wearing and laborious it became for the passage crews and the craft they were manning. As the men's senses numbed, and the only effective antidote, sleep, became less and less possible, a mental numbness set in despite their increased consumption of Benzedrine, which in turn precluded the very sleep they needed. It was in this state that they began the sixth day of the operation, thinking no further ahead than the next duty they had to perform, the next plate of stew they would eat, and the next ventilating period they would use to smoke their next cigarette. Driven by a kind of thoughtless stubbornness that is so often the mainspring of great deeds, and by a dedication born of training, they clung to their tasks as though they needed them to live.

At 0120 that day, X-9, in tow of *Syrtis,* surfaced to ventilate and charge her batteries. After fifteen minutes she dived again, and *Syrtis* gradually increased her speed to eight and a half knots. The craft was supposed to surface again for ventilating at 0300, but Lieutenant Martin Jupp, the commander of *Syrtis,* decided not to bring her to the surface again after so short a spell. At 0907, after reducing speed to five knots, *Syrtis* gave the usual signal—three hand grenades exploded underwater—for X-9 to surface. When there was no response, the tow, another of the three Manila lines used in the operation, was hauled in and found to have parted. Jupp immediately swung round, in an effort to return as soon as possible to where he thought X-9 might have broken adrift. From the log readings and fuel consumption, this was estimated to have happened between 0145 and 0300.

When five more hours passed without any sign of her, Jupp began running through the possibilities—especially the more hopeful ones. Had Sub-Lieutenant E. A. Kearon, passage commander of X-9, made for the Norwegian coast with his crew? They were neither trained to take part in the attack nor in possession of sufficient information to carry it out, but they might at least have made for shore, scuttled their craft, and saved their lives.

The answer came forty-five minutes later, when *Syrtis* sighted a well-defined oil track running in a direction between 088° and 090°, which was the direct course for the slipping position two hundred miles to the north. The four days of porpoising must have prompted the crew of X-9 to fill the forward ballast tank in order to run at a more stable bow-down angle. When the tow parted, the exhausted man at the controls must not have seen the depth gauge and inclinometer bubble in time. The bow-heavy craft must have gone down before the tank could be emptied.

Jupp was kept from informing the Admiralty immediately because *Syrtis* was in an area where it was forbidden to break radio silence. He was reluctant to give up the search, but in such cold waters the men, even on the unlikely chance that they had escaped from the craft before it plunged to the bottom, could not have survived for long. He therefore went north of latitude 70° north, where radio communication with the Admiralty in London was allowed. After transmitting the signal reporting the loss of X-9, he set course for the patrol area, in the hope of being of some assistance to the remaining X-craft after the attack.

Friday, September 17

The remaining submarines, informed by London that additional photographic reconnaissance had shown no change in the disposition of the target ships, were proceeding toward their landfall positions off the Norwegian coast. Both parent and midget stayed below now during the daylight hours, for they were nearing the operational zone. In fact, this was the day the transfer of crews was to take place if the weather permitted, and the passage crews, fortified by the thought, doubled their efforts to get their craft in perfect condition for the men chosen to carry out the mission.

"Change of crew may take place tonight," *Stubborn* signaled X-7 at 0500 that day, adding that the signal to get ready would be four underwater explosions.

In X-7, Peter Philip and the two men under him, J. Magennis and F. Luck, smiled in anticipation of the comfort, the freedom of movement, the hot food, and the undisturbed sleep awaiting them in *Stubborn*'s ample bosom.

"Let's hope the tow holds," Philip said. He had grown so used to the routine that it really didn't bother him much, but thoughts kept popping up of a pint, a bath, a shave, a haircut, and a long sleep.

Stubborn and *Sea Nymph* sighted each other that day and later spoke to each other by S.S.T., a submarine sound-signaling apparatus. Duff was happy to learn that *Sea Nymph* had rejoined X-8. But X-8's troubles had only begun.

Since the change-over of crews, she had been having difficulty maintaining trim. Air could be heard escaping from the buoyancy chambers of the starboard side charge, and as water rushed in to take its place and the charge became negatively buoyant, the craft took on an ever-increasing list to starboard. At 1630, when trim remained difficult even with the compensating tank dry and number-two ballast fully blown, McFarlane decided to jettison the starboard charge. One charge was better than none, he reasoned, and X-8 had, after all, been assigned the smallest of the target ships, the *Lutzow*.

Five minutes later, after setting its timing device to "safe," he released it in about 180 fathoms of water and ordered compensating measures taken to regain the craft's trim.

Set at "safe," the jettisoned charge was not meant to explode. When it reached the bottom it would rest there, a harmless crescent-shaped metal tube whose flooded chambers would become first a curiosity and then a habitat for fish.

But at 1950, only fifteen minutes after sending the starboard charge to the bottom, he and his men were thrown from their seats and knocked against pipes and bulkheads by an explosion that carried through the water with such crushing force that even the men in X-7, beneath the surface over five miles away, thought a ship had been torpedoed, or a depth charge dropped.

McFarlane, only 1,000 horizontal yards from the explosion, was afraid his rudder and hydroplanes had been destroyed, but after trying the controls, he reported to *Syrtis* that the X-craft had suffered no damage. Unfortunately, there was damage to the copper strip that sealed the buoyancy chambers of the remaining side charge. This became obvious only minutes after his report to *Syrtis,* for as the air in the buoyancy chambers escaped, the X-craft took on a list, this time to port.

After trying in vain to compensate for the unwanted weight, McFarlane was faced with one of those decisions that can occupy a man's thinking for the rest of his days. Should he try with this last leaking side charge to carry out the attack, or would the craft's severe list to port and his constant efforts to compensate for it jeopardize the entire mission? If he were forced to jettison the charge in the fjords leading to the target area, and then it, too, like the first, exploded unexpectedly, would the alerted Germans trap the other X-craft taking part?

It took an unusual kind of courage to make the decision McFarlane made—the courage of a man unafraid of being considered a coward. Thinking only of the mission at hand—the enormous concentration and effort that had gone into it, and the men determined to make it a success—he decided to jettison the second charge.

"We'll surface, and to hell with the 'safe' setting this time," he said. "We'll set her to fire two hours after release."

At 1655, after informing Oakley, in *Sea Nymph,* of his intentions, he carefully set the clock mechanism and turned the wheel that released the charge. The craft almost immediately regained its trim as the flooded charge sank to the sea bottom. The tow continued, with *Sea Nymph* increasing speed to nine knots. The plan was to put as much distance as possible between them and the side charge before it exploded. An hour and three quarters later they had covered three and a half miles—more than enough to prevent hull damage from the concussion.

At 1840, the charge detonated, but with a force far greater than the first one had. Both parent and midget were thrown upward by the onrushing water. On board *Sea Nymph,* where several lights went out, Oakley's first thought was of the three men in the much more vulnerable X-craft behind him. He tried in vain to reach McFarlane by telephone. The line was not dead; he could hear static. This meant that X-8 was at least still in tow, however badly she might be damaged.

It was not until several hours later that the telephone line came alive again, and X-8 reported her damage to *Sea Nymph.* The concussion had flooded her wet-and-dry compartment, distorted doors, fractured pipes, and caused short circuits. Almost everything in the craft either functioned poorly or not at all, and beneath the deck boards the water seemed to be rising. The explosion had apparently buckled the seams. She was slowly sinking.

Admiral Barry had been worried about X-8 ever since the parting of her tow three days earlier. Realizing that an X-craft adrift in a rough sea could suffer all kinds of damage, he had sent an urgent message to *Sea Nymph* thirty-six hours earlier, while X-8 was waiting to be rescued. "If you consider it necessary," he had told Oakley, "in the interest of the general security of the operation to scuttle X-8, such action will have my full approval."

After learning of the extent of the damage done to X-8 by the second explosion, Oakley therefore wasted no time in coming to a decision. X-8 could now serve no useful purpose in the operation, and since she might, if sighted on the surface, compromise it, he decided to scuttle her.

"I'm sending you the dinghy," he shouted to McFarlane after heaving to near the crippled craft. "Scuttle her. The show's over."

Sea Nymph then proceeded north of 73° to report back to London and await instructions. She might help the other parent submarines at the rendezvous after the attack or she might, if the attack flushed the *Lutzow* (X-8's target) out of the fjords, torpedo her in the open sea. In any case, she would be there, just outside the minefields off Söröysund, to lend a hand.

"It is not clear why the second explosion caused such damage at an apparent range of 3½ miles while the first explosion, only 1000 yards away, did none," Admiral Barry later wrote in his official Admiralty report. "Both charges had been dropped in approximately the same depth of water (180 fathoms). It may be that only partial detonation occurred in the first charge, which had been set to 'safe.' Whatever the reason, the force of the second explosion would appear to have illustrated the efficiency of the charges. I find it hard to believe that the explosion was in fact 3½ miles away; but whatever the horizontal range was, there is no doubt about the depth of water, so that in any event the result of the explosion was indeed remarkable."

Six X-craft had embarked on the mission, and now, before they had even reached their slipping positions off the Norwegian coast, two were at the sea bottom and three men had lost their lives. If the towing operation could cause such damage, did the mission itself, which still had the intricate German defense system to breach, stand a chance?

10

Sunday, September 19

"Lieutenant Cameron and his crew will board their craft tonight for an attack on the German fleet anchorage. Our prayers and hopes for their safe return go with them."

All officers and ratings had gathered in *Truculent*'s control room opposite their captain, Lieutenant Alexander, for a simple service. Cameron, Lorimer, Goddard, and Kendall, all with ten-day beards, were standing in the front row, and as Alexander paused with the *Book of Common Prayer* in his hand, the only sounds to be heard were the familiar creaky ones of the control wheels being turned to hold the submarine on course. They were now well inside the Arctic Circle; the sea was moderate, the weather mild, and the tow fast. Only an unforeseen catastrophe could prevent X-6 from taking part in the mission now.

This sense that the attack on the *Tirpitz* was certain to happen laid hold of Cameron during Alexander's impressive and moving reading of the Prayer of the Sea. He listened throughout with lowered head, then looked squarely at Lorimer, Goddard, and Kendall, as though the outcome of the mission depended upon how they looked back at him now. All three appeared optimistic, confident, and anxious to get started.

"Is it a pose, or do they really feel that way?" Cameron wrote in his private log. "If so, I envy them. I have that just-before-the-battle-mother feeling. Wonder how they will bear up under fire for the first time, and how I will behave though not under fire for the first time. At least responsible for my share of the operation, I hope. Exercises were fun at Port Bannatyne and Loch Cairnbawn, where if things went wrong, up you popped and came alongside *Bonaventure* for a gin. Feel somehow that gin would be the last thing the Germans would think of in a similar case. If I were a true Brit, the job would be the thing, but I can't help thinking what the feelings of my next of kin will be if I make a hash of the thing."

The transfer of crews was made that evening, two men at a time, before it became pitch dark. Cameron and Goddard were the first to go, and as they boarded the inflated rubber dinghy and began slowly drifting down to leeward on a lead line from *Truculent,* they turned their attention from the final handshakes and good-byes to the sea around them, then to the black shape of X-6 appearing and disappearing at the end of the tow two hundred yards away. Even Willie Wilson, perched on her casing waiting for them, dipped out of sight now and then as X-6 rode down between waves.

Cameron's hands soon became quite numb from the icy spray sweeping inboard, but with his infrared torch he kept signaling instructions back to where *Truculent* lay silhouetted against the lighter horizon to the north. His object was to keep the line of drift down to X-6 as direct as possible, so the dinghy would neither bypass her nor become fouled in her hydroplanes or rudder.

Suddenly they saw the prow of the craft, its peak coming at them from above, and heard Wilson shouting to them. He was clinging to the raised induction trunk with a line in his hand.

"Here!" he shouted, and threw a perfect shot, draping the line across the dinghy's midsection.

Goddard seized it, hauled them alongside, made the dinghy secure to X-6, climbed onto the casing, and disappeared below. Meanwhile Cameron, having signaled to *Truculent* to stop paying out, clambered up to Wilson.

"The starboard charge is beginning to take on water; one of the ballast tanks is slightly cracked; and the periscope gland is leaking. Otherwise everything's shipshape," Wilson said.

He had been living almost without sleep in the tight confines of X-6 for ten days, and now, even in the half-light of the arctic night, Cameron could see the darkened skin beneath his eyes, the lines of fatigue spreading downward from the corners of his nose and mouth.

"Thank you, Willie," he said, finding room in his own anxiety to feel sorry for him. "Now get back to those hot toddies and clean sheets you've been dreaming about. I'll be seeing you in a few days. We'll share notes then."

"Don . . ." Wilson began, but he didn't know what to say. They shook hands as Bill Oxley, of the passage crew, relieved by Goddard, climbed out on deck. Wilson and Oxley got into the dinghy to be hauled, bumping and bouncing, back to *Truculent* on the lead line.

Cameron had been completely mistaken about his crew's optimism and confidence that morning at prayers. Kendall had spent most of the ten days aboard *Truculent* trying to read Somerset Maugham's *The Moon and Sixpence,* but he could not concentrate. The inactivity had made him nervous, given him stomach cramps, and set him to glancing at Lorimer, who always smiled to reassure him and always expected—and indeed waited for—a reassuring smile in return. They were both afraid, and when their turn came to transfer to X-6, Lorimer found something like comfort in the thought that there was a chance of slipping on *Truculent*'s wet deck.

"I can remember almost losing my nerve," he said. "Then the dinghy came alongside the stern of *Truculent,* and after Wilson and Oxley climbed out, I thought I heard air escaping from it. In fact, I insisted it was leaking, but the seaman lending a hand quite rightly assured me that the noise was the water rising and falling over the stern of *Truculent* and running out of the holes in her casing. Once in the dinghy, I felt much better, the seamen wishing me 'Good luck,' and 'See you in two days' time, sir.' "

Lorimer and Kendall had even poorer vision than Cameron and Goddard had had on their trip, and when, suddenly, the tiny craft reared up before them on her tow, they climbed aboard and slid into her, as Kendall later recalled, "like ferrets down a rabbit-hole."

John McGregor, the third member of the passage crew, then went off in the dinghy back to *Truculent,* leaving Cameron and his men to their tight confinement and the tension awaiting them in Norwegian waters. Cameron was already rather alarmed at the craft's list, which he found to be near fifteen degrees, as best he could judge with the craft rolling as it was. This meant that the buoyancy chambers of the starboard charge had much more than a slight leak, and that in the comparatively fresh waters of the fjords, where success would depend on their ability to maneuver the craft, she would be most difficult to handle. Something drastic had to be done without delay, while they were still on the surface and in tow. All surplus food and all but essential gear would have to be thrown overboard and everything else shifted to the port side to offset the list to starboard.

"It was a wrench to see cases of tinned food and orange juice plopping into the ditch, and I hoped that we would never regret the waste," Cameron wrote in his log. "By the time we had jettisoned all we could and shifted the remaining weight to the port side, John had completed his charging and the atmosphere in the craft was refreshed. . . . Then I carried out my own tour of inspection. I was surprised at the condition inside the craft, bearing in mind that she had been lived in for a greater number of days than ever before. Wilson and his crew must have had a field day before handing over. Everything was spic and span; there was very little dampness on the hull, and except for the leak in the top periscope gland, she appeared first rate. The list decreased to 10 degrees when submerged, and one got used to it in time."

Monday, September 20: D day

The four remaining X-craft, still in tow of their parent submarines, had by now all been taken over by their operational crews. *Truculent, Thrasher,* and *Sceptre* had made landfalls and were in their patrol sectors heading for their slipping positions. *Stubborn,* delayed by parting tows but with X-7 still in tow, was approaching her landfall position and would be there on schedule. *Sea Nymph,* having sunk X-8, and *Syrtis,* having lost X-9, were on patrol outside the minefield off Söröysund. Although two X-craft had gone to the bottom and three men had lost their lives, four of the midget submarines had made the passage to the exact position ordered ten days earlier, and that was more than Admiral Barry had ever anticipated. In London his hopes began to rise—prematurely, as it turned out, for the alarms and dangers were only beginning.

At 0300, *Syrtis* sighted a submarine on the surface, quickly identified it as a U-boat, and crash dived. From periscope depth the identifying marks were unmistakable; she was German. Martin Jupp, Captain of *Syrtis,* found her a very tempting target as she drew to within a range of 1,500 yards. She was a sitting shot, a sure hit, and because he had lost his X-craft with all aboard, his mouth was dry with eagerness and tension. But in order not to compromise the operation in any way, the six parent submarines had been forbidden to attack anything below capital ships during passage to or in the patrol areas. Had they been on their return trip after the attack, Jupp would have been free to fire torpedoes at as many enemy ships as he sighted. Now, with his hands gripping the direction rungs of his periscope, he could only watch as the U-boat altered course and then slowly passed out of sight.

As Admiral Barry later wrote in his report: "It reflects credit on our look-outs that with six of our submarines in the vicinity and four of them with X-craft in tow, none were sighted. A single sighting might have compromised the operation, or at least led to anti-submarine activity."

Later that same morning, *Stubborn*, with X-7 in tow, was nearing her slipping position when she sighted a floating mine off her starboard bow. Obviously torn free from its mooring in the same storm that had forced a postponement of the change-over of crews, it came closer and closer, moving from forward to aft with its deadly horns only inches from the hull. After several seconds, during which the men on deck instinctively moved closer to the water, on the remote possibility that they might save their lives by jumping overboard, the mine passed clear, only to get its torn mooring wire caught in the tow astern.

The men waited imploringly for the running sea to free it, but, instead, the sea pushed it down the tow until it became impaled on the bows of X-7. *Stubborn* had by now reduced speed to lessen the pressure of water and the banging of the mine against the craft's bow. Even so, everybody expected any second to see the mine, the side charges, X-7, and possibly *Stubborn* as well, go up in a sheet of flame, for with every dip and roll of the tiny craft the mine was lifted by its horns out of the water and then plopped down again.

What happened then is still talked about by submariners in Britain. Godfrey Place, one of those men who are both fortified and calmed by the tension of others, who thrive on challenge and perform best when performance counts most, stuck his head out the hatch to see what was wrong. The telephone had been disconnected, and the mine, at sea level, with the bow of the craft beaked over it, was hidden from him. It was not until he climbed up onto the casing that he saw the telltale horns, the few feet separating them from the side charges, and what the swirling white rags of sea around them foretold. The craft was pitching and heaving, but he did not hesitate. He made his way to the bow, playing one foot against the other to hold his balance, and stood there in the icy spray, with the wind thrashing his trousered legs and his black hair flying straight back from his scalp, giving the problem his complete and undivided attention.

Just before taking over command from Peter Philip, he had

"borrowed" Philip's boots, and it was with these boots ("enormous, fleece-lined, leather jobs, five guineas at Gieves and the apple of my eye," Philip later recalled) that he reached out, first with one foot and then the other, and delicately tested the mine. From *Stubborn,* he appeared to be trying to shoo it away, as one might a small animal. But it was definitely fouled in the tow, so he tried to submerge the tow in an effort to free it. When this did not work, he turned his attention to the mooring wire, whose torn strands were gripping the tow like fingers.

For the next seven minutes he devoted himself to untangling these strands, and the care he took not to trigger the mine—by hitting it accidentally or shoving it at the wrong time or in the wrong direction—made it harder and harder to go on watching him, and utterly impossible not to. The tension aboard *Stubborn* seemed to pass into him and became something else, something that made his every movement imperative rather than fearful. It was as if the knowledge that his own life and the lives of others depended upon him made everything he did that much more dependable.

Finally, with a calm that was to mark his performance throughout the remainder of the operation, he freed the wire and shoved the mine clear with his foot. A cheer went up from *Stubborn.* Place waved, then shouted cheerfully, as X-7 drifted nearer, "That's the first time I've ever shoved a mine clear by its horns!"

The Attack

11

Monday, September 20

X-6 reached her slipping position that same evening, under a clear sky that grew hazy to the east and disappeared behind low banks of cloud to the west. The sea was moderate, with a long easterly swell, and as Cameron conned the craft at slow ahead toward *Truculent,* which had stopped her engines, the slack of the tow was hauled in by *Truculent*'s crew. He brought the craft to within ten feet of the big submarine's stern, heaved to, and grabbed hold of a line thrown by one of the hands on *Truculent*'s deck. Clambering forward, he made the line fast to the craft's towing bar, disconnected the telephone plug, and rapped the casing twice, thereby signaling Goddard, crouched below in the battery compartment forward, to release the bar. A few seconds later the bar rattled out of the towing pipe, plopped in the water, and was hauled aboard *Truculent.*

"I crawled back to my conning position," Cameron said, "but not before a fair amount of the cold Atlantic had found its way into my boots."

X-6, free at last, then moved slowly past *Truculent,* exchanged farewells, and started in a southeasterly direction around Söröy Island. There was no turning back now, and this knowledge in the gathering darkness added to the loneliness the men aboard the tiny craft shared. The only sound, except for the hum of the engine, was the soft swish of the hull cutting through the polar waters, the only movement the steady climbing up crests and sliding into troughs of swell. Looking astern, Cameron could see *Truculent* as an indistinct smudge turning northward toward her patrol area off Söröysund. All contact was broken; they were on their own.

"I feel very much alone, darling, and cross my fingers," Cameron wrote in his log to his wife. "Can feel Bungey under my waterproof leggings hard against my thigh and am reassured."

Their plan for the night hours was to run on the surface, using their diesel engine and charging the battery at the same time. The quickest course was through a declared minefield, some ten miles away, but because of their shallow draft they thought they would be fairly safe. If a radar-equipped enemy patrol boat appeared, though, and they were forced to dive, it would be another matter.

Cameron, on deck with a life line made fast around his waist, checked with Lorimer on their position by shouting down the raised induction trunk, then settled down to keeping a lookout. Below, the men were slowly accustoming themselves to patrol routine, or at least trying to, against the stimulating knowledge that they were now in hostile waters and not off the rugged but friendly coast of Scotland. Goddard had succeeded in reducing the leak in the periscope gland and was now at the helm; Lorimer worked the controls; Kendall made hot cocoa. Though they spoke little, and only about what they were actually doing, they all shared a heightened awareness of the interior of the craft, its iron dampness, and the way the smell of cocoa and the memory of home became forms of each other in their minds.

On deck, Cameron caught their excitement and added his own, until he felt a chronic throbbing in the craft beneath him. Her spine, sliding straight beneath the sea, was his to straddle; he had the feel of her and he knew he was the master. This was his life, the sea; he had spent the first years of the war sailing through U-boat-infested waters. Now, the idea of his responsibility added to his determination to make a good show of it.

An hour passed quickly as they creamed along through increasingly calmer water. The southwesterly wind had fallen away to a light breeze that hardly marked the surface. This prompted Cameron, who was tired of shouting down the induction trunk in an effort to make himself heard above the din of the engine, to conn the craft and keep his lookout from the wet-and-dry chamber—that is, with his feet resting on the toilet seat and his head out the open hatch. It was warmer there, and if they had to crash dive, he would be able to get below faster.

After traveling two and a half hours in a southeasterly direction, he altered course and started due east toward the coast. The night was wonderfully still, the air sharp, the sky a brilliant scintillation of northern lights. Soon the highland to eastward came in sight, its jutting sectors of rock whitened over with water. Suddenly, as though someone had struck a match at the end of a tunnel, he picked up one of the running lights of a small craft close inshore to the northeast, about three or four miles off. Blacked out as they were, there was little danger, but he kept her under observation until she passed out of sight where the peaks of Söröy Island darkly loomed, as obscure in the starlight as an upcoming storm.

They were still over three hours' traveling time from the coast, and he was beginning to feel cold and hungry.

"John!" he yelled. "Come up and relieve me. I need something hot."

Nothing could have pleased Lorimer more. He had never been this far north before, much less this close to the coast of Norway. With great alacrity he climbed into the wet-and-dry chamber and squeezed up on the toilet seat next to Cameron.

"Keep an eye out for Godfrey and Henty," Cameron said. "They should be close by somewhere. We're heading straight for the minefield and I'll relieve you before we get there."

With the induction trunk sucking in air to feed the diesel engine, Cameron found the temperature inside the craft almost as low as outside. Still, it was a pleasant change to sit on a comfortable seat, and he could, while sipping hot cocoa, warm his feet on the gyro motor. He was only halfway through his first cup and in the middle of checking on their position when Lorimer came clambering down with the mission's first alarm.

"Ship's lights in sight to northwards!"

The men went to their panic stations, stopped the engine, and prepared to dive, while Cameron went up to investigate.

"Sure enough, there was a light low down on the horizon, but it was quite a distance off," Cameron wrote in his log. "I watched for a while through glasses until it suddenly dawned on me that it was a star. What a relief!"

Tuesday, September 21

At midnight, when Cameron took over from Lorimer, the moon was high enough above the horizon to glisten on the snowdrifts ahead, where the jagged cliffs shot up around the entrance to Stjernsund. This was a narrow funnel of water roughly twenty miles long and a little over a mile wide, with gun batteries and torpedo tubes covering its entrance and an extensive minefield forming a barrier across the water leading to it. The Admiralty's intelligence reports had been scant as to the type and depth of mines in the area, but here and there, as they started over the outer rim of the mine barrier, Cameron could see "floaters" that suggested ordinary shallow-water mines. Having no idea where the mine-swept channels leading to the entrance were, he was careful to stay outside the hundred-fathom line, where the Germans would naturally have laid most of their mines against ocean-going ships and submarines. Aside from hoping that no mines had been laid at depths shallower than the X-craft's draft, there was really nothing else he could do. The tide was coming in, and that helped, for every increase in the depth of water added to their chance of passing through unscathed.

As they neared the inner rim of the mine barrier, and moved into the safe water used by coastal vessels, their timing could not have been better. The short arctic night was coming to an end, and the stars to eastward were slowly disappearing in the lightening sky. A fresh offshore breeze had sprung up, raising a choppy sea and whipping up crests of spray. It was devilishly cold, though, even in the comparative shelter of the wet-and-dry chamber, and Cameron did not know how much longer he could stand it. He nevertheless kept checking his bearings, trying to make the most of the faint light rising in the east before dawn forced them to dive. The land ahead showed up now as a jagged black wall, with the entrance to Stjernsund a narrow gray chasm and Söröy Island, to the north, a series of gleaming peaks. Along the shore, where twigs of stunted arctic birch showed black against the snow, there were thousands of rocks awash on either side, the wind around them sending up a spray that obscured the entrance and made it appear farther off than it really was.

He glanced at his watch, which showed 0200 hours, and shouted down the hatch: "Down in about fifteen minutes, men. We'll trim down now."

The induction trunk was lowered, their position fixed as accurately as possible, and the gyro checked. Though they were still three miles from the entrance, Cameron wanted to avoid even the slightest chance of their being spotted by enemy observation posts on Söröy or in the mountains to the south. Closing the hatch behind him, he went below, where the motionless air created the false but nevertheless exquisite impression of warmth. The other men were in fact almost as cold as he was, though not nearly as wet and stiff.

They ran on the surface for a few minutes while Cameron changed into long flannel underwear, dry clothing, white woolen socks, and tennis shoes, and hung his wet gear in the engine room, which had come to resemble a "Chinese laundry." Then he pressed the diving Klaxon and ordered depth and speed. Down at sixty feet they caught a reasonably dependable trim and headed straight for Stjernsund at two knots. The list was now about ten degrees, but the craft handled well, so Cameron could relax and enjoy the hot meal that Kendall had prepared for him: beef bouillon, lamb's-tongue, string beans, potatoes, and, for dessert, loganberries with tinned milk.

At 0400 he brought the craft to periscope depth, but the periscope was so foggy that he had to go back to sixty feet to strip it down and clean the eyepiece. Fifteen minutes later, at periscope depth again, he saw that they were right at the entrance to Stjernsund, about half a mile from the north shore. The incoming tide, sluicing between the cliffs on either side, was so swift and strong that the surface resembled that of a river running over rocks. He anticipated some difficulty in maneuvering, and wanted at all costs to stay away from the sunlit southern shore, where even at a depth of sixty feet they might be spotted by a plane or helicopter. Very carefully he set a course that would take them through close to the north shore, where the craft would be in shadow all the way and he would not be dazzled by reflections on the water if he had to come to periscope depth for any reason.

With the tide behind them they passed through quickly, hoping that they were not alerting anyone on watch or setting off a sonar alarm. They kept listening for signs of danger—the sudden starting of a patrol boat's engine, for example—while moving so close to the north shore that Cameron could see it above him through the side viewing port. They waited until they were about a mile past the entrance before going up for another look.

Returning to periscope depth was probably the most hazardous operation inside enemy-occupied waters, and as an added precaution, before going up all the way, Cameron searched around with their small, passive, hand-rotated sonar. But like all the X-craft commanding officers, he found it too time-consuming and, in the back of his mind, he knew that when the action started he would take his chances with the periscope itself.

At any rate, the sonar reported nothing, so he slowly raised the periscope until an inch or two of it showed. The surface was flat and smooth now, and as he scanned it, encompassing the entire area, it occurred to him that he was looking as much for the periscopes of the three other X-craft as he was for enemy patrol boats. Though he would not know it until later, mechanical troubles soon put X-10 out of the running. She successfully breached the outer barriers and came to within three miles of her target, the *Scharnhorst*, but was then forced by crippling defects to return with her side charges to her parent submarine off the Norwegian coast.

Cameron was of course more immediately concerned about X-5 and X-7, the two others assigned to the *Tirpitz*, but except for antiaircraft-gun positions on top of the hills, there was nothing in sight. The periscope was still far from clear, and if it had not been for the strong contrasts of light and shadow on the water, he might have had trouble fixing his position and setting a course.

Back down at sixty feet, they continued eastward along the shadowy north shore in the hope of reaching the inner end of the sound, where it formed right angles with Altafjord, in about nine hours. This would give them time to recruit their energies for what lay ahead. Cameron set watches, pairing himself with Kendall, Lorimer with Goddard.

"Two on and two off," he said. "That way we'll all be rested by the time we reach Altafjord. And to make things even easier, we'll use 'George.' "

"George" was the automatic helmsman, but it soon broke down. Even after Goddard had worked on it for over an hour, it refused to function, so they were forced to steer by hand. Counting the leaking side charge, the leak in the periscope gland, and the crack in the ballast tank, this was the fourth thing to go wrong. Though no one grumbled, the mechanical failures added to the slow attrition they were being subjected to. They could sleep, eat, and build up their energy, but their endurance, after all, was inseparably tied to that of their craft —or would be if and when they got past the antisubmarine net into Kaafjord.

12

Tuesday, September 21

During the day they sighted several more antiaircraft-gun positions in the hills, and once, when Lorimer was on watch and his curiosity brought him up for a peep, he saw an enemy patrol boat at anchor on the south side of the sound where the distance from shore to shore was well over a mile. He felt a momentary flush of excitement, but the boat showed no signs of weighing anchor, and since they were hugging the north shore, they had no difficulty in passing by undetected at sixty feet.

It was a glorious day, with the water a deep blue and the snow along the shore stretching clear down to the tidemark. There were no tracks in it and no signs that the water ever became rough enough to wash it away along the edges. Indeed, except for the evidence here and there of Germans in the hills, the place looked deserted, although once Cameron saw a small farmhouse, with smoke coming from its chimney, a nearby barn, and racks for drying fish stretched out on the beach below. The chimney smoke, disappearing almost as soon as it reached the cold crisp air, was the only sign of life, but for Cameron there was something detaining and poignant in the scene. Waiting an extra second or two before lowering the periscope, he looked again, one final time.

At 1200 he brought the craft to periscope depth again and fixed his position, which he calculated to be a mile and a half from the eastern end of the sound. It was still bright and sunny, with a light westerly breeze, no sea, and no signs of traffic. To save time he altered course from east to south by southeast and headed diagonally across the mouth of the sound for Altafjord, the large inner basin of the sea with fingers of water stretching through the mountains in all directions. To the south lay the Brattholm Islands, and it was here, in among these bits of glacial drift in Altafjord, that they intended to spend the night before the attack.

The tension was increasing now, for they were deep inside enemy waters, where even the slightest possibility of detection had to be avoided. They remained below for four hours, until 1600, and even then, when they returned to periscope depth and Cameron saw the onset of darkness on the water and no signs of surface craft, they went below again, for two more hours, running at the same depth and speed, in order to make as little noise as possible during their approach to the islands, some six miles away.

When they went up for another look at 1800, Cameron saw Tommelholm, one of the larger islands in the Brattholm group, just visible ahead as a dark blob. It was still too dangerous to remain at periscope depth, though, so he brought the craft down to eighty feet and conned her closer. Half an hour later he brought her to low buoyancy for an all-around look through the night periscope. They were now only four miles from Kaafjord, where the *Tirpitz* lay, and all around them were German occupation troops, harbor guards. Their hearts pounded as Cameron carefully opened the hatch and climbed onto the casing to investigate. There was no surface traffic, but lights were burning brightly in the town of Alta and at the destroyer base at Lieffsbotun.

"All clear," he whispered down to his men. "Let's bring her in closer. Easy now."

Conning the craft close inshore to a small brushwood cove, he ordered the motor turned off and then remained there on the casing, sending his imagination batlike into the dark around him while the men below prepared for the night's activities. It was one of those untarnished evenings that seem to exist only in the high latitudes: the air was free of the slightest particle of dust; the sky appeared almost reachable. Gradually, as the pupils of his eyes widened, he could see clumps of snow that flurries of wind kept disturbing. Except for these flurries, the stillness was extraordinary; like the cold air nipping into his beard, it seemed to permeate everything—even his excitement. Never in his life had he heard wind so clearly as he heard it now. The snow swirls made seeing it work almost indistinguishable from hearing it blow. This is how wind blows, he thought, when there's no one around to hear it.

It was a world where the water, and even the land, had a withdrawn, secretive quality, where everything permanent and fixed had been given a flowing form by the snow. No oddity of rock or terrain was recognizable as such. There was just the unaccented snow itself, which made the tiny craft something like a floating home. He could hear the stern pawing the water in response to the movement of the men below, and that sound, too, like the sound of the wind, seemed in some strange way to be related more to silence than to sound.

This powerful sense that he wasn't really there, that the silence and desolation of the place had nothing to do with him, the mission, or whether or not it succeeded, brought everything together—the soft lacing of wind in his ears, the icy water washing over the casing and passing in and out of his tennis shoes, the cold air penetrating the pores of his woolen sweater—and made it one with his own elation and alarm at being there on time, in the Arctic, exactly where he was supposed to be, without the Germans knowing it.

Suddenly, the door of a small hut opened less than thirty yards away. A blaze of light crossed the snow and water; men were talking. Cameron stood there, wild-eyed, trying to think what thought could not think, unable to swallow and afraid to breathe. They were talking in voices free of the slightest suspicion that anyone was listening, and this only added to the feeling he had that his ears were not his own, or that he was listening from somewhere else. They were where they were, but where was he?

Then the door slammed. The darkness returned, and, with it, the stillness that made it easier to believe that nothing had happened than that something had. His knees were still shaking when a small vessel came round a point on the island, keeping close inshore. This being a more expected danger, it actually helped him to recover from the unexpected one. Within seconds, he was down the hatch and ordering the men to dive, regaining his sense of command in the act of putting it to use. Half an hour later he brought the craft back to the surface, only to be sent almost immediately down again by another vessel, proceeding in the opposite direction.

"Movement seems to start with the night in Norwegian shipping circles," he said as they waited below for the second boat to pass. "Thank God they burn navigation lights."

When the sound of the boat's engine receded into silence, he brought the craft up again and motored down to the lee of Tommelholm, where a stretch of rocky shoreline, too steep to hold snow, effectively camouflaged X-6's black casing. As this was the rendezvous position, he kept looking along the shoreline for Place and Henty. Their orders did not require them to meet before the attack, but they had all expressed a desire to, and Cameron would have been delighted and encouraged to see them and know that they, too, had made it at least this far.

Had he taken the unnecessary and foolish risk of motoring around the island, he would have seen them, for they were both there, Place, in X-7, around a bend on one side of him, wondering where he and Henty were, and H. Henty-Creer, in X-5, behind a point of land on the other side of him, wondering where he and Place were. They were within a few hundred yards of one another, preparing for an attack that each imagined he alone was left to carry out. Indeed, when a sudden outburst of star shells and searchlights from the destroyer base at Lieffsbotun lighted up the sky, at 2100, Cameron was convinced that the others had been spotted. But then when he heard no alarms and saw no further action taken, he wondered, then hoped, then wondered again. Were Place and Henty and their crews there, somewhere, in the darkness, doing the same thing he and his crew were doing?

From an intelligence report he had been given just before the change-over of crews, he knew that only a few miles away, probably in the town of Alta, there were Norwegian Resistance men at work. He had never met Karl Rasmussen, Torstein Raaby, or Harry Pettersen—and indeed he never would—but it was their report, flashed to the Admiralty in London and then to the parent submarines, that he had been given: the *Tirpitz*'s sound-detection equipment was to be overhauled and her guns dismantled and cleaned on September 22. There would of course be several destroyers, all with operating sound-detection equipment, in Kaafjord along with the *Tirpitz*, but it was encouraging to know that the *Tirpitz* would not be listening tomorrow.

Cameron sat on the casing looking at the brilliantly floodlit antisubmarine net at the entrance to Kaafjord three miles away. Would they get through the next morning undetected and then make it under the antitorpedo nets to the side of the *Tirpitz*?

The headlights of a car twisting and turning along the snow-banked shore road caught his attention. They were powerful lights, with an oval shape that suggested a chauffeur-driven limousine—a Rolls-Royce, perhaps, of 1938 vintage.

"I thought it might be carrying Admiral Oskar Kummetz," Cameron said, "and sat there speculating on his reaction the next day if all went well. The moon was rising above the mountains and everything was brushed with silver. Was Eve watching it back in Scotland? Was Iain behaving himself? I felt very homesick. The elation of sitting in the middle of the enemy's fleet anchorage vied with the feeling of a small boy very much alone and wishing to go home and be comforted. I wasn't conscious of fear, just of wanting someone to talk to."

As midnight approached, a fresh breeze swept in from the north, and the sky clouded over, blotting out the moon and whatever small chance they might have had of being seen.

Cameron had Lorimer relieve him and went below to take stock of their position.

Wednesday, September 22

"I remember being on deck watch at midnight," Lorimer wrote later. "It was the most extraordinary, unreal feeling. There we were bang in the middle of the main German naval base charging our batteries, doing running repairs, and listening to the BBC over our own wireless—and no one knew we were there! The whole base was easy to see as there were no darkened ships. The *Scharnhorst* had moved into Altafjord for target practice; we could see her less than a mile away, and the *Tirpitz* in the distance in Kaafjord as a blurred mass of lights. It all seemed so unreal, too good to be true. . . . There was a considerable amount of sea traffic, mostly small drifters taking men ashore, and we were forced to dive several times to avoid detection. Eventually we got very close to shore, and as we were against a cliff, we gave no silhouette."

Cameron had, meanwhile, rooted out his attack orders, made sure of every detail, and put a match to them. It was his intention to leave the Brattholm Islands at 0130 that morning in order to give Kendall, the diver, plenty of time to cut through the antisubmarine nets at the mouth of Kaafjord. Although the three X-craft taking part in the mission were to operate independently of one another, there were periods when they could release their charges under the *Tirpitz,* and periods when they were forbidden to release them. These prearranged periods were designated "attacking" periods, when it was safe to place bombs under the *Tirpitz,* and "firing" periods, when it was unsafe to do so. In this way each midget would avoid being blown up by the charges of the others.

The first attacking period started at 0100 that morning, and lasted seven hours, followed by the first firing period, lasting one hour, from 0800 to 0900. From then on each attacking period would last three hours and each firing period one hour.

Just to be on the safe side, Cameron released the charge

connections to avoid any possibility of their jamming the next morning. Then he set both firing clocks to the six-hour setting. He wanted that much time to escape after releasing the charges under the *Tirpitz.* The clock in the flooded starboard charge worked perfectly, but each time he set the switch on the clock on the port side, the fuses blew. He tried the five-hour setting, and the fuses blew again, then the four-hour and three-hour settings, with the same result. Only at two-hour or less settings did the clock function.

"I was left with a flooded charge set to six hours," he said later, "a charge that would probably, for all I knew, fail to explode, and a perfect charge with a maximum setting of only two hours. Supposing the perfect charge operated. It didn't leave me much time to get clear. My idea was to attack at 0630, lay my charges, and run for it. Given two hours I might possibly, if all went well, just make it through the antisubmarine net at the mouth of Kaafjord. If so, I'd have the whole of Altafjord in which to elude the inevitable hunt. If not, I'd be penned in in the narrow confines of Kaafjord and could look forward to a sticky time."

He was pondering this when Lorimer called him up on deck. There was a brightly lighted passenger vessel close on their port beam. She was carrying Norwegian prisoners taken at Spitsbergen two weeks earlier, but they did not know that. In any event, there was no danger of their being seen, because they were under the lee of the island.

"I'll take over now, John," Cameron said. "Tell Dicky to have a hot meal ready for me when I come down at 0130."

The night had turned very cold, with the wind whipping spray over everything. Cameron tooled the craft to a more sheltered part of the island and managed to wedge the bow between two rocks, where they lay out of the wind. He kept hoping to make contact with the other two craft, but there was no sign of them.

"I had to make up my mind what to do next," he recalled. "With one charge flooded, a defective clock, a very unreliable periscope, an air leak in number one ballast tank, a nasty list to starboard, and very little ballast water to play with if Kaafjord proved to be much fresher that Altafjord, our situation was tight indeed but by no means impossible. If I went in to attack and succeeded, only one of my charges might explode, but the gaff would be blown and the enemy on the lookout for Godfrey and Henty. If I waited for a day, the others could carry out their attacks and I could limp around and perhaps do a little damage afterwards. That way, if the others were in the fjord and in a fit state to operate, I would not compromise them. If the others were in the fjord? But they had not turned up. They might be in a worse plight than I. Besides, if I waited any longer, my periscope might be completely unserviceable and an attack out of the question. What was I to do?"

Whether from desire, determination, the soundness of his reasoning, or the knowledge that the *Tirpitz*'s sound-detection equipment was to be overhauled and her guns dismantled and cleaned that day, he suddenly shut the hatch behind him, went below, pressed the diving Klaxon, and headed for Kaafjord and the *Tirpitz*.

13

Wednesday, September 22

"The feeling of excitement was intense," according to Cameron. "I had some orange juice brought into the control room as I felt we might need it when our mouths got dry."

They had left the Brattholm Islands at 0145, dived to sixty feet, and were proceeding by dead reckoning toward Kaafjord. The control room had been cleaned up and everything movable stowed away. Cameron had changed into dry socks and another pair of tennis shoes and was sitting on the gyro enjoying the cocoa and hot stew that Kendall had prepared for him.

"As far as my crew was concerned, everything was on top line," he wrote. "If the present weather held—low clouds, rough sea and occasional showers—it would be ideal for the attack, especially in view of the fact that I was going to have to use my defective periscope more than I normally would. Our trim was quite good and John was handling her superbly."

For months they had practiced cutting through antisubmarine nets, and now the net that counted was only three miles away. Dick Kendall did not wait for orders from Cameron; he went to the battery compartment, got his rubber diving suit, and, in the cramped space just forward of the periscope, began struggling into it. Goddard and Cameron helped him in silence, allowing the firmness of their helping hands to say what they were thinking. Their eyes met occasionally as they worked, but they said nothing, not even when Kendall, suited and ready, squeezed past them with his net-cutting gun and breathing apparatus and climbed into the wet-and-dry chamber.

It was Cameron's plan to conn the craft slowly up to the net at a depth of about forty feet and keep her there, pushing ever so slightly against the steel mesh at a speed of about one knot. Goddard would by then have climbed into the battery compartment forward to observe the net through the net periscope —a stubby affair designed to observe a net at close quarters. At the same time Lorimer would be carefully controlling the craft's depth, speed, and trim to make things easier for Kendall when he climbed out and began working his way forward along the hull.

There was no doubt that the flooded periscope, the leaky side charge, and all the other mechanical failures had added to the tension the men were under, but they had trained themselves to so keen a pitch, they were so close to their objective, that the setbacks actually added to their determination to carry on. Kendall, sitting on the head in the wet-and-dry compartment, waited in silence for the order from Cameron to leave the submarine. When that order came, he would shut the door and begin flooding the chamber by opening a valve controlled by him from inside the chamber itself. The water would come from an internal main ballast tank directly beneath the chamber, and later, on his return, the same water would be pumped back into the main ballast tank. In this way the craft's depth and equilibrium would be retained, but, more important, no air bubbles would be created to alert German patrol boats plying the waters above. For the same reason, his net-cutting gun was powered not by air pressure, which would have sent telltale bubbles to the surface, but by water pressure, which in water told no tales.

The engineers had in fact thought of everything except how to make the claustrophobic loneliness of the wet-and-dry chamber a routine experience. Kendall had flooded escape chambers a hundred times during training, but, like every other diver connected with the mission, he had not learned to enjoy the process.

As diver George Honour, Godfrey Place's former roommate, put it: "You're shut up in a space about the size of a water main with a lid over your head. You sit there, cold and lonely, waiting for the water to come up. You long for it, but you can't let it in too fast because there's a limit to what the body can stand. It takes about four minutes, and then when you're completely covered and all the air is gone, the force on your body terminates in a sudden, final squeeze as the pressure inside equalizes with the pressure outside. It's like a nasty kick in the head from a mule."

Only after this "nasty kick" would Kendall be able to open the hatch, climb out into the water, and make his way along the slippery hull to the bow. At that point he would clamber down the net to the craft's keel and proceed to cut the net strand by strand upward in a vertical line until the craft, nosing against the net with a headway of one knot, began to slip through.

But even then Kendall's job would not be finished, for as the craft moved slowly forward, he would have to walk with the net's loose strands to the after end of the craft to keep them from becoming snarled in the hydroplanes, propeller, and rudder. Then, at the last minute, as the stern slipped through, he would have to make sure he had a firm hold on the craft, so as not to be left behind. He would hitch a ride, so to speak, and then climb back into the chamber, shut the hatch, and pump the water back down into the main ballast tank.

"You can close the hatch when you first get back in," Honour explained, "but you can't lock it closed until the pressure inside is a little less than the pressure outside. That's what gives you the return kick, and it's just as nasty."

By 0400 the sun had risen over the mountains and was glistening on the surface of the water, which had, unfortunately, calmed and was now as flat as glass. They were less than half a mile from the net between them and Kaafjord, and inside the craft the tension, or, rather, the accelerated breathing it caused, was burning the oxygen supply at twice the normal rate. No one spoke as Cameron ordered the craft brought to periscope depth. He had seen a patrol boat and a ferry with a white funnel during his last look, and he wanted to check their position. But when he raised the periscope to eye level, he could see only a green film. Except for a tiny hole in the top left-hand corner of the eyepiece, he was looking through water. The periscope had flooded again, this time to the point where he was almost totally blind.

"Down to sixty feet," he said. "Flooded periscope."

In the silence that followed, as he removed and cleaned the eyepiece, he could see from the dejected look on the others' faces that they did not want the mission scrapped any more than he did.

"We had waited and trained for two years for this show," he said later, "and at the last moment faulty workmanship was doing its best to deprive us of it all. There might be no other X-craft within miles. For all I knew, we were the only starter, or at least the only X-craft left. I felt very bloody minded and brought her back to her original course. . . . It might not be good policy, we might spoil and destroy the element of surprise, we might be intercepted and sunk before reaching our target, but we were going to have a very good shot at it."

Nearing the net again at thirty feet, he heard the propellers of a ship passing over them and immediately went to periscope depth. The glass remained clear just long enough for him to see the stern of a trawler. She was heading straight for the net, which could mean only one thing: the gate had been opened—was open—for her to pass through.

"We might be able to get through behind her," he said.

But at periscope depth they would be blind on the one hand and too slow on the other. Their electric motor would never propel them through the water fast enough; the gate would close again before they reached it. Their only chance was their London bus engine, which operated only on the surface.

"Surface!" cried Cameron. "Full ahead on the diesel!"

Kendall, waiting in the wet-and-dry chamber for the order to leave the craft, could hardly believe what he clearly heard Cameron say. However daring it was for him to leave the craft to cut through the net, it did not compare with trying to pass right through the gate on the surface. "The plan was a little too bold for my taste," he said. "I felt it would be safer to cut through the net than take the risk of revealing our presence."

But Don Cameron had made his decision, and his failure, his refusal, to show the slightest hesitation was despotic. So successfully did he control his own emotions that the rest felt constrained to do the same. He allowed them time only for the responsibilities of the moment, the actual duties they were expected to perform. He might have been alone, so they followed him, apprehensive but faithful.

Within minutes the craft was following in the trawler's wake, and she was small enough, her deck was flat enough, for her to be taken for almost anything. Seen from shore she would probably have looked like a raft being towed across the mouth of Kaafjord. But no one saw her, or, if someone did, nothing was done about it.

"We're through!" Cameron cried. "Dive!"

He smiled, remembering something he had been told but had only half believed at one of the many briefings he had attended in Scotland: that the German garrisons in the remote areas of Norway were low-grade troops whose morale had been softened by long months of isolation, inactivity, and homesickness. Laborers, farm hands, dishwashers, and petty clerks mostly, they had been drafted into Hitler's army and then used as occupation troops in relatively safe areas such as the far north of Norway, where, with nothing to do, no female companionship to enjoy, and no chance of being furloughed home, they could only wait for the war to end.

"It was fantastic luck," Kendall said. "The crew on the trawler and the men on guard at the net booms must have been either drunk or blind."

All the same, they had made it. They were in Kaafjord, with the mighty *Tirpitz,* lying still in the glassy water, less than three miles away.

But their periscope had flooded again, and before they penetrated the last barrier—the antitorpedo nets around the

Tirpitz—Cameron wanted to see what could be done about it.

"Down to seventy feet," he said.

This time Goddard stripped it down, poured out the water, dried the prisms, and reassembled it. But since the leak was outside the hull, at the top of the periscope where the welding had fractured during passage, there was really nothing they could do about the flooding of the bottom prisms except to dry them and then go back up to periscope depth for a look before they flooded again.

Ironically, one of the special features of the X-craft was its periscope, which was so thin at its upper extremity that it hardly rippled the surface of the water. The Admiralty engineers had naturally been aware of how unruffled the surface of a Norwegian fjord can be on a calm day, and they had made the X-craft periscope a thing of slender beauty for that reason. But a thing of slender beauty cannot always withstand the pressure and pounding of 1,000 miles of ocean, and now here was X-6, in unruffled Kaafjord, with her greatest asset rapidly becoming her greatest handicap.

With the bottom prisms dry again, Cameron wasted no time in going back up to periscope depth for another look, and this in fact was the last all-around look he had. The fjord was fairly crowded with German warships of every size, and about two miles away, between them and the *Tirpitz*, a tanker lay at anchor with two destroyers refueling alongside.

It was profoundly impressive and moving, like watching lions feeding, to observe them from so close a distance. They were the enemy, but the refueling of ships in harbor was such a familiar and relaxing sight, especially to an experienced seaman like Cameron, that for a moment they might not have been. There was a sailor, for example, fishing over the side of one of the destroyers, and the peaceful aspect of it suddenly appalled Cameron in the light of what they had come to do. It was as if he had the sailor in the sights of a long-range rifle that he suddenly wished contained no bullets. He did not want the sailor to die; he wanted him, instead, to catch a fish. He even, to his own surprise, felt a strange and secret kinship with him.

Why are we here? he wondered, as though something illusory were on the verge of becoming real. Without realizing it, he was falling prey to one of the dangers of penetrating an enemy's defenses—recognizing similarities—then questioning, undermining, his reason for being there. But soon he shook himself free and went on with the job. Within seconds he set a course to pass astern of the tanker, ordered a depth of thirty feet, and proceeded to strip down the periscope again.

They were running now by dead reckoning, and the snow-fed layers of fresh water in the fjord were making it difficult for Lorimer to keep the craft in trim. One minute they would be passing through a patch of salt water, and the next minute through a layer of fresh. Since the salt water was denser than the fresh, the X-craft was more buoyant in the salt than in the fresh. Lorimer had to compensate for this difference in weight by using the pumps. In the salt water he had to pump water into the ballast tanks to prevent the craft from rising, and in the fresh water he had to pump water out to prevent the craft from sinking.

He knew how much Cameron hated using the pumps, for they made the kind of noise a destroyer's hydrophones could detect. God, somebody's going to hear us, he kept saying to himself. But what could he do? The fresh-water layers were everywhere, and if did not use the pumps, the craft would porpoise through the water. The men would not be able to work on the periscope at all.

"With so many enemy ships about," Lorimer said later, "it was imperative to use the pumps, motor, and hydroplanes as little as possible. You tried not to vary your speed, but sometimes you had to. The hydroplanes had less effect with less speed, and in an emergency you had to increase your speed to make the craft respond quickly and efficiently. And yet the more noise you made, the better your chances were of being detected from above."

At a speed of two knots, it took them over an hour to reach the position estimated by Cameron to be astern of the tanker.

He decided to return to periscope depth for another look, but no sooner did he put his eyes to the glass than he saw—only a few yards away—the camouflaged hull of a destroyer. They had come up between her bow and her buoy, and the cable was only inches away. It was about to rip off their periscope.

"Dive! Sixty feet!"

It was at times like this, when the tension was greatest, that the lives of the men depended on John Lorimer. His operation of the controls had to be not only accurate, but also kept at a minimum. There was no time for mistakes, much less for correcting them.

At sixty feet they turned everything off, drew the external steel shutters over the glass viewing ports, and waited. Had some German sailor on the hydrophones heard them? Were patrol boats speeding to the scene? Imagining what might be happening above them, they waited for the first depth charge to explode. No one said a word, and as the seconds passed, the silence took on personality. They become aware of the slightest roll and movement of the craft, the wash of water in the bilges, and even the feathery touch of fish against the hull. There was a somber eloquence in her sounds suggestive of the fear all submariners have of being trapped below, where the iron sky you throw your last words to throws them back.

"We're all right," Cameron said after a few minutes had passed. "No activity. Nothing." He withdrew the shutters from the viewing ports. "Slow ahead."

14

At a steady two knots they headed for the last obstacle between them and the *Tirpitz*—the antitorpedo nets. Though they had tools powerful enough to cut through these nets, they had no intention of cutting through them, because according to British Intelligence the nets around the *Tirpitz* extended down fifty feet in water as deep as 120 feet. There would therefore be ample room for them to pass beneath the nets both on their way in and on their way out.

"Periscope depth," Cameron said.

They were getting so close that from this point on, besides the enemy's active and passive sonars, magnetic devices, patrol craft, and even hovering helicopters, there would be the human eye to contend with—the sailor leaning over the side of his ship, the officer on his way to shore, or the man on watch whose job it was to report anything suspicious. This made using the periscope more hazardous, but Cameron had no choice. With all the fresh-water layers, conflicting currents, and mechanical difficulties, he simply could not conn the craft all the way in by dead reckoning alone.

They were near the north shore of the fjord when he put his eyes to the glass, and as he turned the lens toward the southeast, where the *Tirpitz* lay, the sun's reflection on the water almost blinded him. He could see the dark form of the ship and her shadow on the water, and just as he was about to turn his attention to the net buoys around her, the periscope hoisting motor short-circuited. There was a loud noise and a flash of light as an electrical fire started; the control room filled with smoke.

"Sixty feet!" shouted Cameron.

Blinking their eyes against the smoke, twisting and crouching to reach this or that extinguisher or control, they were so highly trained they did not have to decide what to do or be told to do it. Finally, with the fire out, the damage checked, and the smoke passing into the other compartments, they felt an almost drunken temptation to lie down. The atmosphere was heavy with stinking fumes, dampness, and heat, and it was through this almost palpable gloom, with burning eyes, that they looked at one another. The periscope-flooding was getting worse, the hoisting motor had burned out, the port side charge was flooded, they were sending up a trail of air bubbles wherever they went, and the fifteen-degree list was increasing to the point where it was almost impossible to move about.

They had done their best and seemed to have failed, or, rather, their midget had failed them, and now time was running out. They hated the idea of aborting the mission, and illogically hated themselves for thinking of it. But if they did not escape soon, or at least before the first firing period started at 0800, when the bombs of X-5 and X-7 might explode, they would almost certainly be trapped in Kaafjord and destroyed by depth charges. If they could slip back out through the antisubmarine net to Altafjord, they could wait until darkness, scuttle the craft, climb the mountains bordering the shore of the fjord on the east, and make their way to Sweden.

They had everything they needed for the trip: mountain-climbing gear, walking boots, warm clothing, compasses, Chinese-silk maps of the Swedish frontier, Lugers, medical preparations and bandages, tiny saws for use if a frost-bitten finger or toe had to be amputated, considerable sums in German, Swedish, and Norwegian money, and huge chunks of tobacco to barter with the Lapps for food.

But besides their fear of being trapped in Kaafjord, there was another fear, which no one mentioned. Just behind the mountains above Altafjord there is a desolate plateau that stretches for hundreds of miles to the south, east, and northeast, into Sweden, Finland, and Soviet Russia, where it skirts the narrow lowlands of Petsamo and then extends eastward again to the White Sea and the vastness of Siberia. When under snow, it is a featureless wilderness with endless horizons, icebound valleys, barren hills, and a free-running wind whose relentless thievery of the body's heat makes it fiercely hostile to human existence—an uninhabited, storm-swept world where the chances of snowblindness, exposure, and death by freezing far exceed the chances of survival.

Even with maps and compasses, Cameron and his men could lose their way, for the area has never been adequately charted, and no map shows more than a vague outline of such distinguishable landmarks as bluffs, bogs, lakes, and ravines. The terrain, mostly a confused and baffling network of almost identical little hills and valleys, all of them rippled in the same way with wind-driven snow, not only could destroy a sense of direction, but also make it almost impossible to keep a straight compass course. At the Swedish border itself, there was nothing except cairns at intervals of miles, so that they could cross over into freedom without knowing it, without seeing road, sign, or house, and then trudge on until they were hopelessly lost in the endless forests on the Swedish side. Their only real hope, if they decided to make the attempt, would lie with the nomadic Lapps, who knew nothing about compasses or maps but who were able to cross the dreadful desolation of the plateau in winter. Lapp families did it twice a year, with their herds of reindeer and their reindeer-drawn sledges, just as their ancestors had before there were countries, much less borders to separate them.

What did the men think? Cameron turned to them. Did they want to carry on or turn back toward Altafjord and the possibility of escape to Sweden? He was no more suicidal than they were and their lives were not his to squander. What did they want to do?

No one wanted to be the first to admit defeat, and as they

exchanged glances in the claustrophobic gloom of the control room, something like torment webbed the air and made it hard to breathe. Their position in Kaafjord was becoming more untenable by the minute; they knew it and wanted to escape, but they also felt a nagging reluctance to exchange familiar dangers—dangers that they had been trained to expect and overcome—for unfamiliar dangers that might overcome them. What it came down to was that, as sailors, they found the overland journey to Sweden more inimical than the *Tirpitz* and her 2,400-man crew.

Besides, to turn back now was inconceivable; they were so close—less than five hundred yards from a ship they had come to destroy. There was also the enormous realization of what they had accomplished so far in getting into Kaafjord, and the exhilarating, almost unbelievable fact that despite their mishaps and mechanical failures they were still as undetected by the Germans as the herring swimming past their viewing ports. If they remained undetected by sonar and unseen by the human eye, they could overcome the mechanical difficulties and maintain the initiative. Their side charges, once released beneath the *Tirpitz,* would explode, and that was what they had come to accomplish.

It was John Lorimer, without whose superb work at the controls they would never have gotten this far, who broke the silence. "Lets see what she's worth, Skipper," he said.

Cameron looked at him, then at the others, and suddenly it was as if their laboring craft had given them a desperately needed object for their tensions and fears. The unforeseen, after all, was what they had trained themselves for months to overcome.

Cameron smiled. "Slow ahead, John," he said. Then, to Kendall: "Dick, you'll help me raise and lower the periscope from now on. Meanwhile, let's dry the prisms."

They moved closer, skirting the northwest shore about four hundred yards off the port bow of the *Tirpitz.* At one point Cameron was about to come to periscope depth when a dark shadow appeared overhead. An ominous scraping sound followed, so he stopped the motors to investigate. Through the starboard viewing port he could see the bank of the fjord rising above him and a few fish nosing about. But what interested him more was a black shape, like a pontoon, with wires hanging from it.

Cameron did not know it, but Norwegian patriots had tried to cripple the *Tirpitz* in another fjord by rolling depth charges down the bank into the water, and this contraption was the Germans' answer to such sabotage attempts. But as Cameron said later, he had not the "foggiest idea" what the contraption was; it just looked "rather nasty."

X-6 did not appear to be caught on anything, though, so he decided to move off into deeper water and go up for another look. The glass was very fogged, but he could just make out dark blobs which he took to be the net buoys.

"Slow ahead at sixty feet," he said.

But at that depth, instead of passing beneath the nets, they rammed into them. They went down to eighty feet, and the same thing happened. Then down to one hundred feet—same thing. Finally, they went to the bottom, and Cameron, looking through the net periscope up forward, said, "They go right down to the sea bed!"

British Intelligence had been misinformed about the anti-torpedo nets around the *Tirpitz*. In point of fact, the outer net extended from buoys on the surface to about one third of the way down; the middle net, held by wires attached to buoys on the surface, started one third of the way down, where the outer net ended, and extended two thirds of the way down. The third or inner net was anchored to the sea bed and held in a vertical position by floats attached at intervals to its upper edge. Though these floats remained submerged, they had sufficient buoyancy to stretch the net upward to where the middle net ended. The Germans, in short, realizing that buoys could not have supported the tremendous weight of a single net extending all the way to the bottom, had ingeniously devised a three-net overlapping system whereby each net did one third of the work.

Cameron, a seaman whose ideas were mostly based in experience, had always believed that if you are ready to give up everything to the solution of a problem, you will always solve it. Kendall could climb out of the craft in his diving suit and cut through the nets, but these were the most formidable anti-torpedo nets Cameron had ever seen, and there was no telling how long it would take, even with every bit of luck, to cut through them.

Quickly he rose to periscope depth to check the boat gate. It was close to shore, so close, in fact, that only boats of shallow draft could pass through. No ocean-going submarine could possibly have made it, so the German guards would probably not be looking for a submarine there. This thought no sooner occurred to him than he saw a picket boat about to go through on her way to *Tirpitz*'s side. If they swung round and got in the boat's wake . . . They had done it once; they could, they might, do it again.

It was as if all the mishaps and bad luck stimulated some reserve of determination he did not know he had. He set a course and cried, "Full ahead! Surface depth."

The foaming water of the picket boat's wake was washing over them; they were right behind her, at the gate, scraping and bumping against the bottom, but passing through, nonetheless —in broad daylight.

Cameron ordered a quick change of course into deeper water and gleefully cried, "Dive, dive, dive!"

He had taken a look on their way in and thought he had seen the Germans closing the boat gate behind them. He was mistaken, but when he told his men, Goddard turned from the helm and said, "Well, we've had it, then, as far as changing our minds."

Thirty-five hours had passed since they had cast off from their mother submarine, and for most of that time they had been submerged. Exhaustion and tension had taken their toll, but there was no time to rest, let alone wipe down the condensation or strip the periscope again. It was 0705, which meant they had to be as far away from the ship as possible in fifty-five minutes to avoid being blown out of the water, for if either X-5 or X-7 had succeeded in placing their bombs under the *Tirpitz,* those bombs would be timed to go off between 0800 and 0900.

After one last look up the sun's dazzling path at the *Tirpitz,* Cameron decided to make straight for a position under her stern to drop his first charge. He was about to alter course to port when, with a dreadful crash, they rammed a submerged rock. He was thrown against the gyrocompass and Kendall nearly knocked off his feet as the craft, shooting upward at an angle of sixty degrees, broke the surface only two hundred yards from the port side of the *Tirpitz.* As their fright gave way to concentration and effort, they went full astern and slid off into deeper water, but before they did, Kendall, back on his feet, saw sunlight streaming through the viewing ports. How could they not have been seen?

15

They had in fact been seen, by a flak petty officer aboard the *Tirpitz,* who happened to be standing by his battery on deck just above the officer of the watch, an old friend of his.

"Hey, Hein!" he cried. "A long black thing just popped up over there. Looked like a submarine!"

This was at exactly 0707, two minutes after X-6 had entered the anchorage.

The officer of the watch, Chief Petty Officer H. Valluks, shouted back, "Where?"

"Over there by shore. Abeam of us."

"You're dreaming. How could a submarine get in our net cage?"

"I tell you I saw it."

"It was probably a dolphin."

"But there was a hatch."

"A hatch, eh? What about a conning tower?"

"No, she had no conning tower."

"Then you'd better have your head examined. A submarine without a conning tower!"

"Listen, Hein, I'm not crazy."

"You must be. Do you know how shallow the water is over there? A submarine would have to burrow its way through the *rocks* to get in."

The men aboard the *Tirpitz* had spent nine long months in the snowy hush of Kaafjord, and during that time they had been constantly warned to be on the alert against sabotage and put through innumerable practical exercises to test their alertness. Captain Heinz Assman, second-in-command under the handsome and soft-spoken Captain Hans Meyer, had been almost fanatical in his determination to prepare the crew for any and every eventuality. He had devised one scheme after another, discussed them with Captain Meyer, and then, with the Captain's approval, put them into effect.

"We sent air bubbles up alongside the ship from an air hose, for example," Meyer said later. "We had all kinds of oddly shaped things emerging alongside. We found ways to shake the antitorpedo nets around the ship and had men go below and hammer against the hull. We made all kinds of noise both beneath and above the surface. Boulders were rolled down from the side of the fjord in imitation of actual sabotage attempts by the Norwegians in an anchorage farther south. With great secrecy we had dummy frogmen made, then brought them to the surface near the ship. We even lashed the dummies to logs and had the logs slowly drawn toward the ship during the day and night.

"And whenever we did these things, the guards always sounded an alarm, until one alarm led to another and then finally all alarms became unpopular. Sleeping men—and the ship contained hundreds at any given time—had to respond each time because they had no way of knowing whether or not it was an actual attack. They were then expected to return to quarters and go back to sleep, but it wasn't easy."

To make matters worse, the men, alerted to the point of desperation by "Assman's tricks," as they were called, began overreacting to things they might otherwise have correctly ignored. This led to a series of false alarms that had nothing to do with Assman's planned alarms. It was a case of German thoroughness outdoing itself and then backfiring.

"Why was no alarm sounded?" Meyer went on. "Well, I think we had too many false alarms, and whenever someone on watch sounded a false alarm he was laughed at, made a fool of, by his comrades. The sailors used to call it 'to go mad' when someone sounded a false alarm. There was no question that those who sounded them were commended by their superiors, but this was not really honored by the men. The sailor is educated to take things in stride and think everything over twice. He doesn't like to act with undue haste. I am positive that this contributed to the fact that the sighting of the midget at 0707 on the morning of the twenty-second of September, 1943, was not taken seriously."

Meyer then unwittingly touched upon one of the great contributions made to the X-craft mission by the Norwegian Resistance, in particular by three of its members in the nearby town of Alta: Karl Rasmussen, Torstein Raaby, and Harry Pettersen. The Norwegian women hired to work in the galley aboard the *Tirpitz* had been dedicated readers of the ship's bulletin board. They had memorized precisely the weekly duty roster and passed the information on to Rasmussen and Pettersen, who in turn passed it on to Raaby. The result was that the British Admiralty knew the day before the X-craft slipped their tows off the Norwegian coast that the sound-detection system aboard the *Tirpitz* was to be overhauled and the guns dismantled and cleaned on September 22. The commanding officer of each X-craft, informed of these two facts before taking leave of his respective parent submarine, had naturally made the twenty-second his target date.

"The sound-detection units of the ship were operated continuously save for short overhaul cycles or repairs," Meyer said. "Unfortunately, this was the case on the twenty-second of September. I doubt, however, that our sound-detection unit would have been able to detect midgets in the light of the ship's own noise. The guns were being dismantled and cleaned that particular morning, so there was noise along the entire length of the ship. But these midgets must have had a very low noise level anyway. Otherwise they would have been detected by the guards at the entrance to Stjernsund, or by the patrol boat in Stjernsund, or certainly by the destroyers in Kaafjord. If I remember correctly, there were five destroyers, widely separated, acting as advance protection for the *Tirpitz*, in Kaafjord on September 22. On the other hand, nobody on the German side ever imagined that enemy midgets would be used over such enormous distances and then turn up in Altafjord and Kaafjord."

Under the circumstances, it was no wonder that after the flak petty officer aboard the *Tirpitz* sighted and reported X-6, he deferred so quickly to the doubts of Chief Petty Officer H. Valluks. Why should he be the one "to go mad"? Perhaps it *was* a fish. Or a log. Or another of Assman's tricks.

Had this sighting been reported immediately, at 0707, when X-6, crippled and floundering, was two hundred yards away, it would have been possible for the Germans to blind her by smoke-screening the entire fjord. They could then have put their many detection devices to work and dropped enough depth charges to destroy a dozen midgets.

16

But the alarm had not been sounded, and down in X-6 Cameron waited, his mind's eye on the ship above him, a puzzled look on his face. What could have happened to the eyes of the men on watch aboard the *Tirpitz*? Why weren't depth charges being dropped around them? The collision and the sixty-degree bow-up angle had destroyed both the gyro and the magnetic compasses. The compass needles swung wildly; the men had no idea which way they were heading. Indeed, about the only thing they managed to do was stay under water.

Glancing at his watch (it was 0709), Cameron ordered the motors started and, at half speed, at a depth of seventy feet, steadied on what he thought was a course parallel to the west side of the fjord. If they were, as he estimated, approximately one hundred yards from shore, they would strike the stern of the *Tirpitz* in about two minutes. At that point they would slide down along the hull of the ship, release their first bomb under the keel where X turret was located, and crawl forward under the keel to release the second under B turret.

If all went well, and X-5 and X-7 had been able to release their bombs in the same way—fore and aft, in accordance with the Admiralty's plan—the success of the mission would be complete. With all bombs going off together, as they were designed to do, the ship would be raised simultaneously at both ends. Her back would be broken just as surely, and in the same way, as an ear of corn can be broken when it is bent at both ends.

Cameron "crossed his fingers" and waited. But after nothing

happened in three minutes, he went to periscope depth for another look. X-6 was now laboring in the water, heaving and rolling like a wounded whale, and despite Lorimer's efforts to control her, she broke surface again, only eighty yards abeam of the battleship. Though again they had no way of knowing, there was now no longer any doubt among the *Tirpitz* lookouts that a submersible of some kind had penetrated the net cage.

"I was in my cabin in the stern elevation deck," Captain Meyer recalled. "I had just had breakfast when my first officer, Captain Wolf Jung—Assman had flown to Germany to take over command of another ship—came in to report that one of the lookouts had seen something like a small submarine inside the nets."

According to the official log of the *Tirpitz*, this second sighting was made at 0712, a full five minutes after the first sighting. Even then, though, the alarm was not immediately sounded.

"Jung and I looked at each other rather unbelievingly," Meyer went on. "We came to the conclusion that this surely was another false alarm. It was pleasant to know that the men were so alert. Still, I felt it only proper to sound the alarm and get everybody to his fighting post and the ship ready for action. The First Officer disappeared, and a few seconds later the alarm was actually sounded."

According to the log, the alarm was sounded at 0720, eight minutes after the second sighting, and thirteen minutes after the first.

"The report of the suspicious object in the water passed a whole chain of echelons before the alarm was sounded," Meyer said. "This explains why minutes passed before the matter was taken seriously. It would have been proper for one of the two officers on duty to sound the general alarm immediately after the first lookout reported seeing a submarine inside the nets. Why wasn't it sounded? Too many false alarms."

From the German point of view, this thirteen-minute delay was bad enough, but worse by far was the kind of alarm that finally was sounded by the man in charge of the alarm system on the bridge. Whether he had become peacetime conscious or just plain jittery as a result of Assman's alertness tricks, he sounded five short blasts—an alarm that did not exist in wartime. Crewmen, justifiably confused, looked at one another. Was it the real thing or another trick? Five short blasts constituted an order for the men to go to their "watertight-door positions." If the ship had struck an iceberg, the order would have made sense. But they were anchored in ice-free Kaafjord, and besides, watertight doors were closed automatically in response to a general alarm.

Meyer explained that instead of sounding the one long blast for general alarm and *then* five short blasts, to indicate that a submarine had been sighted, the man on the bridge in charge of the signal system lost his head, "went mad."

Meanwhile, the men in X-6, unaware of the confusion above them, were tensely awaiting some response from the battleship and, at the same time, literally feeling for her underwater. Cameron had seen her momentarily on surfacing, so when he set a course in her direction and brought the craft down to below her keel depth, he kept looking out the viewing ports above him in an effort to get a glimpse of her shadow like a cloud overhead. When that shadow appeared, he would order the motor to be put astern, to stop them directly below the battleship's center line, then bring the craft slowly up until it rested, like a fly on a ceiling, on its own special antennas, which could be raised or lowered from inside.

They struck something, and for a second he thought it was the *Tirpitz*. But they were below her keel depth. With a sickening feeling in his stomach, he decided it was the antitorpedo net on the ship's exposed, or starboard, side. He was mistaken; they had struck some loose wires hanging from the battleship's port side, and they were now caught in them. The men, their exhaustion turning to sloth, were close to desperation now. The smell of grease, oil, machinery, and sweat had made a compost of the place. The air hung heavy in the compartments; there was no flurry or waver other than that of heat itself. Yet they were still together and still alive, and as their bleary eyes met, it was this source of encouragement that they seized upon.

The shackle of the spare towing pendant at the craft's bow was entangled in the wire. When Lorimer tried to break free by going forward as far as possible and then astern as fast as possible, the wires held. Finally, when they did break loose, the craft shot to the surface out of control, and as the water cascaded from the viewing ports, they saw a huge gray mass above them. It was the *Tirpitz,* only sixty feet away, and from the rail crewmen were shooting rifles and throwing grenades at them. The hours-long danger of being sighted had at last ended —with actually being sighted. They were more depressed than surprised, saddened at the thought that what they had feared and half expected and even prepared themselves against had at last come about and could not be altered.

Even under the circumstances, though, that towering gray hulk was a stunning thing to see, for not once during their many months of training in Scotland had they imagined themselves seeing her from this distance, through their viewing ports, in broad daylight. She stretched for hundreds of feet fore and aft until it seemed there was nothing else there but the giant ship, the upward-plunging walls of the fjord, and their tiny craft in between.

Had the distance been greater, the guns of the *Tirpitz,* frantically reassembled by the alerted men in the turrets, would have blasted them out of the water. But they were below the angle of depression of these guns; their tiny craft was too close to the most powerful battleship in Europe for that battleship to use her power. This seemed to add to the rage of the Germans as they aimed their rifles and threw their grenades. The bullets bounded off the steel casing and skimmed off over the water; the exploding grenades banged like hammers against the highly explosive side charges.

"Dive!" cried Cameron. "Dive!"

Being sighted and shot at had one unexpected result: it completely destroyed the insidious temptation they had felt earlier to give up. They still had their bombs, and now more than ever they had the will to use them.

Their bow had veered toward shore, so Cameron went half astern and backed the craft down under the ship's keel. Nothing could touch them there, but neither could they remain there. It was already 0720, and if X-5 and X-7 had released their bombs under the ship, these would be going off in forty minutes. They could hear the growing tumult above them, the grinding of gears, and the clash of metal against metal. The entire ship had come alive, and above the din Cameron shouted that there was no chance of their escaping now. They were walled in by the barren mountains above them, by the closed nets around the ship, and by thousands of alerted German troops along the shore.

"Even if we can get out of this net cage," he said, "the net at the mouth of the fjord will be closed. We're hemmed in, and there are five destroyers outside this net cage just waiting for us to try to escape. So we'll release both our charges here under B turret and go up and scuttle her."

The time was 0722. He set the charges to go off in one hour and ordered them released. The two crescent-shaped bombs fell away from the hull, rolling slightly but throwing up little mud as they came to rest directly under the battleship's keel.

Cameron did not know it, but twelve minutes earlier, X-7 had also set her charges to go off one hour after being released. She had just released her first charge only yards from where X-6 had released both of hers, and was at that moment moving aft, flylike, under the keel, to release her second charge under X turret. The two craft had been towed through miles of ocean and had penetrated many defenses, yet here they were placing their bombs under the *Tirpitz* within minutes of each other. X-5 was also at that moment in Kaafjord. She was still over two miles away, however, and had not yet penetrated the antitorpedo nets around the *Tirpitz*.

Thus all of the X-craft chosen to attack the *Tirpitz* had succeeded in getting into Kaafjord on schedule. The timing was extraordinary, but it had a drawback: it placed X-6 within six feet of three two-ton bombs, one of which was set to go off earlier than the two she had released. Since the first bomb to explode, X-7's, would almost certainly detonate the other two, six tons of amatol would be exploding, earlier than the men in X-6 expected, right next to where they were lying.

Even without this awesome knowledge, Cameron was as anxious to escape as his men were. He and they knew that the timing device on their port side charge had been defective since they left the Brattholm Islands. It might detonate the charge in one hour, as it was set to do, but it might also detonate it in fifteen, ten, or even five minutes.

Never before in their lives had time been so important. But before they could surface and abandon ship, there were maps, charts, and secret documents to be burned and special equipment to be destroyed. The British Admiralty had made a strong point of this, so that no X-craft would jeopardize the chances of any other. If X-5 and X-7 had already laid their bombs and were on the way back to their parent submarines off the Norwegian coast, for example, the Germans, with X-6's maps, charts, and documents in their possession, would know how and where to intercept them.

When Cameron gave the order to destroy everything that had to be destroyed, they all worked in earnest to get the job done. They were intent and almost brutally efficient at the task, and yet, despite their desperation and frantic haste, they could not help making mental notes about the craft in which they had trained and lived together for so long. Now that they were about to abandon her it was as if they were seeing her after a lapse of years. They could pinpoint odd areas of space here and there where they had rested, eaten, or stretched their legs. There were the gauges they had stared at for hours, the wet clothes with which they had made a "Chinese laundry" of the battery room, and the always renewed glistening beads of condensation. And there was the strange poignancy of the gluepot in which they had heated their stew and soup. It was as if what mattered, what they were really being forced to relinquish, was not the craft so much as the hours of struggle and sacrifice they had shared inside her.

Lorimer tried to swallow one secret document that had become too wet to burn, and while working up enough saliva to get the first page down, his eyes came to rest on the two chronometers. Still ticking away, they represented the mission too vividly, he felt, to be left. "I just couldn't see leaving them behind, so I slipped them in my boot."

The smoke from the burning maps and charts added to the already intense heat and stench. The men sweated so profusely that water dropped off their ears and ran from their hair down their necks. They wanted to get out and breathe air again, that same cold air they had pulled into their lungs around the Brattholm Islands. Even if it meant being shot and killed, they wanted once more to breathe fresh air.

"We'll surface now and open the sea cocks," Cameron said. "John, as we abandon ship put the motor going astern with hydroplanes to dive."

17

Seven minutes before Cameron's decision to scuttle the craft and surrender, several German sailors, under Lieutenant "Tiger" Leine, had run down the ship's port gangway to a motor launch. Armed with rifles and grenades, they were awaiting the chance to cripple the craft and take her in tow.

Suddenly, like a geyser, X-6 broke the surface less than fifty yards away.

"Who'll go first?" shouted Cameron against a hail of rifle fire. The bullets bounced off the steel casing where the hatch protruded slightly above the craft's raftlike deck. Without a doubt, the first man out stood the greatest chance of being killed—whether by accident or intention on the part of the Germans.

"I'll go," Goddard said.

"Hold your hands up," Cameron said, "so there'll be no mistake."

The Germans immediately held their fire when they saw the hatch open, however, and, swinging alongside, made the tow fast. They would capture the crew as well, Leine reasoned, and bring them aboard for questioning.

Goddard climbed out, followed by Kendall. Then came straight-backed Lorimer, his breath steaming, his sweaty beard tingling, in the cold arctic air. All were wearing the British submariner's thick white sweater, which showed no insignia or rank. With heads erect they stepped into the motor launch in that same order.

"We didn't even get our feet wet," Kendall said later.

Then wiry Cameron, his steel-gray eyes shot with red, climbed out. The mission had made cereal of his body's fiber; he felt weak and dreamy and could barely tense his muscles. But it was not until he stepped into the motor launch, until he relinquished his command, that he noticed these almost comforting infirmities.

For some reason they all felt a strange reluctance to talk—even to one another—now that they were in German hands. They had slipped into Kaafjord without being seen; now it was as if they wanted to be taken captive without being heard. Besides, this was German-occupied territory, so they were in a sense guests. The ingrained British belief that it was up to the host to start the proceedings and set the tone was perhaps strengthened by the way German sailors along the ship's rail kept shouting down at them. Some actually looked as though they were bursting with good news: their arms waved, their grimaces looked like smiles, and they seemed to be screaming "Wait'll you hear this!" in German. Lorimer watched them, appalled and spellbound for a moment, a part of his mind wondering what the news could be, another part thinking they were overdoing it a bit.

Meanwhile, X-6, with her sea cocks open, her motor going astern, and her hydroplanes in dive position, was moving away, taking up the slack in the towline between her and the launch. Exactly as Cameron had planned, she was moving back down under the ship on top of the side charges they had just released. More than that, she was about to pull the motor launch down under with her.

"Cut the line!" Leine cried to his men. "Cut it! They've scuttled the damn thing!"

Once free of the sinking submarine, the motor launch swung round and tied up at the battleship's port gangway. Cameron and his men were ordered aboard, and up they went at gunpoint toward the quarterdeck. Lorimer happened to be a step or two ahead of Cameron, and just before he reached the last step he turned and made what Kendall considered the best remark of the whole trip, and one typical of John.

"Skipper," he said, "shall we salute the German flag?"

Cameron, snatching at the irony and humor of it, answered, "Why, of course!"

According to the *Tirpitz* log, the four prisoners were taken aboard at 0725, or about three minutes after they had released their charges under the ship. Captain Meyer was still in his cabin, putting on his coat and hat before going to the bridge.

"Before I had left the cabin," he said later, "the First Officer came to tell me that a small U-boat had come to the surface within the net box, that four men had abandoned this U-boat and that the boat had thereafter gone under."

Meanwhile, the first four Britishers ever to board the *Tirpitz* were standing at attention on the quarterdeck like dignitaries on an official visit. At Cameron's order, they saluted and, despite their exhaustion, bloodshot eyes, and unkempt beards, carried it off confidently enough to become objects more of curiosity than of hatred.

When Cameron explained that they were British, the Germans at first refused to believe him. How could such a small submarine travel the more than 1,200 miles from Britain, they wanted to know. Cameron and his men naturally had no intention of answering that. They were thoroughly searched, and their belongings—keys, pistols, wallets, chocolate, photographs, cigarettes, and chunks of tobacco—were laid out in individual piles. In Lorimer's pile were his two watches and the X-craft's two chronometers. Each one, as it was laid down, told the same story: less than forty-five minutes remained before the charges were to explode.

He glanced at Cameron, who appeared somehow incomplete without his pipe, then at Goddard and Kendall. Though they were not allowed to communicate with one another, it was obvious that they shared the same dreadful suspense. If X-5 and X-7 had already laid their bombs and escaped, would the simultaneous explosion of twelve tons of amatol break the ship's back, detonate her magazines, and start a series of explosions and fires that would destroy not only the ship but everyone on it?

Suddenly, with one long blast, the general alarm sounded. According to the ship's log, this came at 0736, twenty-nine minutes after the flak petty officer had first sighted X-6, sixteen minutes after the mistaken peacetime alarm had been sounded, and at least five minutes after the four prisoners had been taken aboard. It corrected the earlier alarm of five short blasts and ordered the men to their action stations, the raising of steam, and the readying of the ship for sea.

"The *Tirpitz* was designed in accordance with the old traditions of the sea," Chief Engineer Alfred Eichler said later, in an interview. "Traditions derived from sailing-ship days, when the gentleman was separated from the commoner. The crew, that is, was quartered 'before the mast' and the officers 'aft of the mast.' This meant that no one, whether officer, noncom, or seaman, slept near his action station. My quarters were over 150 yards from the tech center where I was to report when a general alarm sounded."

Therefore, when the general alarm sounded, most of the 2,400 men began climbing up or down ladders, running fore or aft or athwartship, and in every direction on deck. They had already responded to the peacetime alarm. Was it the real thing this time or another false alarm? Since most of them had been below in the vast honeycombed interior of the ship, they had no way of knowing.

It was no wonder that the British thought panic had overtaken the ship shortly after their arrival on board. Indeed, what added to their uneasiness was the feeling of being cut off from participation in the feverish activity arising from their capture. They had laid their bombs, but now they were immobilized, unable to help or hinder the outcome, like condemned men who had in a sense condemned themselves. Glancing nervously at one another, they finally began to make their German guards nervous.

"Why didn't you attack?" they demanded. "You English are

dummkopf. You get this far and you don't even use your torpedoes!"

But Captain Meyer, on the bridge, knew something was wrong, and although his first impulse—to move the ship out of the net cage—was the correct one, his hands were tied.

"The ship was not ready for sea," he later said. "She had no steam. The general alarm included the 'raise steam' order automatically, and therefore no order to this effect had to be issued. But even an accelerated 'raise steam' would have taken a full hour. There were no tugs. In short, it was impossible to leave the net cage immediately."

He was nevertheless convinced that his ship was in danger where she was, so while steam was being raised he came to some quick decisions.

"Not knowing how the midget was armed," he recalled, "I had to figure on torpedoes, magnetic mines, or ground mines. I discounted torpedoes because the constricted space inside the net cage would not have allowed the midget to maneuver properly or escape destruction when the torpedoes exploded. I therefore had to consider either magnetic mines or ground mines, and immediately ordered the diving equipment brought up from below and two divers prepared. But as it always took time to get the men suited and the equipment ready, I meanwhile had the entire hull checked with long poles. This 'hull scratching' was not very promising, though, because nobody ever really got to the bottom. It was more like stabbing in the dark."

While this "hull scratching" was being carried out, Cameron and his men, lined against a bulkhead facing eight Germans with Tommy guns, were intently watching the diving equipment being brought up on deck. It was apparent to all of them that the Germans were going to search for bombs beneath the ship and then, if they found any, try to diffuse them. Cameron knew that with so little time left they did not stand a chance. When two divers, without much enthusiasm, started over the side, he stepped forward and tried to dissuade the officer in charge from sending them.

"They'll be killed," he said.

The divers were sent over the side anyway, "to be blown up," Cameron and his men thought. There was a launch alongside the ship, but the prisoners were too far from the rail to see it. The divers climbed down into the launch to prepare their equipment, not down under the ship as the prisoners thought, "within feet of tremendous bombs whose clocks were ticking away."

On the bridge Captain Meyer was not waiting for the results of the divers' search. He was convinced that ground mines had been laid beneath the ship, and, as he later explained, "There was only one thing to do against ground mines: move the ship from where she was—that is, at least one ship's width away from her present position. X-6 had been scuttled on the port side, abeam of B turret forward, so it was urgent that the ship be moved to starboard."

Because there were no tugs available, he issued orders to have the bow shifted to starboard by means of the ship's two anchor chains. These anchor chains formed a V at the bow of the ship. The shift to starboard could therefore be accomplished simply by taking up on the starboard anchor chain while slacking off on the port. Trouble lay in the fact that the anchors were relatively close together, so that the shift to starboard would be minimal at best.

At the stern, matters were much worse, and Meyer knew it. Gale winds that often swept through the fjord had necessitated securing the stern to land with eight heavy mooring cables. These cables would have to be slacked off, laboriously raised over their mooring posts, dragged to other mooring posts to starboard of the ship, and then taken up again. The procedure would take well over half an hour, and there was no way of knowing when the ground mines—if the British had indeed laid any—would go off. !

It remained Meyer's intention to move to another anchorage as soon as steam was raised, but meanwhile something was happening beneath the surface, just off the ship's starboard bow, that was soon to alter that intention.

X-7, trying to escape after releasing both her side charges under the ship, had become entangled—for the fifth time since entering Kaafjord—in the nets around the ship. Her earlier difficulties with these intricately devised nets had already knocked her gyrocompass off the board and put her trim pump out of action. Without a compass, Godfrey Place had no exact idea of where they were. They had used two air bottles, and only 1,200 pounds were left in the third. Their charges were due to explode in less than forty-five minutes, not to mention X-5's and X-6's, which might go off any time after 0800. Every second counted, and they were caught in the nets again, this time at a depth of sixty feet.

"A new technique in getting out of nets had by this time been developed," Place said later. "The procedure was to go full ahead, blowing economically, and then go full astern; the idea being to get as much way on the boat as the slack of the nets would allow and thus have a certain impetus as well as the thrust of the screws when actually disengaging from the net."

Place had been trying this new technique for fifteen minutes when suddenly, at 0740, X-7 broke free, shot to the surface, and was seen, sliding over the top of the net between two buoys, by *Tirpitz* lookouts. The four prisoners on deck saw her, too, and as the ship's machine guns splattered her with bullets, they noticed something that *Tirpitz* lookouts were not trained to notice. Both her mine clamps were empty, which meant that she, too, had laid her side charges beneath the ship. Therefore at least eight tons of amatol would be going off sometime after 0800.

The men in X-7 were in an even worse predicament than Cameron and his men, despite the fact that they had just slid over the top of the net and were seemingly in the open water of Kaafjord, where they at least stood a chance of escaping. As Place later recounted: "I did not look at the *Tirpitz* at the time as this method of overcoming net defenses was new and absorbing. But I believe we were at the time on her starboard bow. . . . We were too close, of course, for heavy fire, but a

8 TONS OF AMATOL !

large number of machine gun bullets were heard hitting the casing. Immediately after passing over the nets all main ballast tanks were vented and X-7 went down 120 feet to the bottom. The compressor was run again and we tried to come to periscope depth for a look so that the direction indicator could be started and as much distance as possible put between ourselves and the coming explosion. It was therefore extremely annoying to run into another net at 60 feet."

They were caught again, less than fifty yards away, and time was running out.

18

The sighting of X-7 sliding over the net brought about a complete change in Captain Meyer's plans. It was now apparent that there might be several midget submarines in Kaafjord, all of them waiting with torpedoes for the *Tirpitz* to leave her net cage. He saw clearly the bind he was in and issued several orders in rapid succession: catapult one of the ship's four planes off for submarine reconnaissance; close the boat gate in the nets to prevent other midgets from passing through; interrogate thoroughly the two top-ranking prisoners from the scuttled midget; and, finally and most urgently, accelerate the movement of the ship within the net cage "at least one ship's width away from its present position."

The bow of the ship was still in the process of being moved to starboard and the stern still being readied for moving when Cameron and Lorimer, each guarded by two armed crewmen, were taken below, to separate cabins, for interrogation. It was now 0800, only minutes before their bombs were set to explode; below decks was the last place they wanted to be.

"You was born, yes?" the German interrogator asked Lorimer, who correctly interpreted the question to mean "How old are you?"

Whether it was because Lorimer's bearded face might have been taken for that of a Norwegian or because of the surplus of timepieces found on him earlier, the Germans had planted two photographs of Norwegian patriots among his belongings. Having seen them do it, Lorimer was prepared for whatever the Germans had in mind. Moreover, before starting on the

0812 !

mission, the crews had been briefed on what to say and what not to say in the event they were taken prisoners.

"Say nothing about the X-craft," Lieutenant Commander Newton, a British submariner who had been a German prisoner of war, had said. "Nothing about the mission, its objective or the number of men involved. The interrogator will chat with you about your family, English literature, the English countryside—and then casually slip in a question like 'What was the weather like in Portsmouth when you left?' hoping that you will correct him and say, 'We didn't leave from Portsmouth.' "

With this particular interrogator (the fluent one had gone with Cameron), that kind of friendly chat was out of the question. Lorimer told him his name and rank, was surprised when the two planted photographs were not produced, and thereafter maintained a stony silence. Meanwhile the time for the explosion was drawing near, the clocks were ticking away, and the fascination of watching the trap being sprung blinded him to the danger it posed to his own life. He waited, trying desperately to appear calm while the skin around his ribs became almost unbearably tight, like a vest he had had to empty his lungs to button. It was as if all the force in the world were gathering there in Kaafjord beneath the giant battleship. The atmosphere seemed to contract. Lorimer could not breathe, his heart pounded, his palms turned moist.

At exactly 0812 he was thrown high out of his chair and onto the steel deck. The *Tirpitz* was lifted seven feet by two explosions in rapid succession. The three bombs up forward exploded simultaneously, with a surge of water so great that the ship oscillated like a steel whip for several seconds. In the forecastle, the teak deck buckled; men working on the anchor chains were hurled about, as one of them said, "like bits of paper." A sailor on deck was catapulted into the air and killed instantly when he landed on his head against the chain cable; others up forward suffered broken limbs and fractured skulls. !

The underwater pressure fanning outward and upward was so tremendous, it moved so fast, with such shattering power, that the fourth bomb, farther aft, was detonated only seconds later. The crew had been unable to move the stern in time. There was a hole the size of a barn door in the hull on the port side of the keel under X turret, and already the ship was listing to port. At the bow, which had been moved as much as the anchor chains allowed, there were buckled plates. Just before all the lights went out, there were deep internal tremors, as from an earthquake, through the entire length of the ship. Then came the hiss of steam, an acrid smell from short circuits, and the roar of inrushing water.

"Complete chaos followed," said Kendall later. He had remained with Goddard on the quarterdeck after Cameron and Lorimer had been taken below for questioning. "My knees buckled as the explosion hurled the ship out of the water. . . . The ship started to list rapidly to port. Steam gushed from broken pipes. Seamen ran in all directions. Oil flowed from the shattered hull and covered the water of the fjord. Injured men were being brought up on deck. Machine gunners imagined they saw submarines everywhere, and their fire mingled with the din of hand arms. It was impossible to take it all in. All around was confusion. . . . I suddenly felt tired to death, yet with a wonderful feeling of relief."

Officers seemed feverishly to be piling orders, counter-orders, and activity between themselves and their anxiety. One had reached the point where he was no longer concentrating on how to prevent further destruction to the ship but on the destruction itself. There were so many buckled doors and twisted pipes that he could not decide which damaged area demanded his special attention.

The ship's entire supply of beer had exploded and her fire extinguishers had broken open, spattering everyone near with white foam. The man guarding Goddard, literally covered with foam, appeared on the verge of becoming someone else. He seemed to realize at last that the British had succeeded in bombing the ship, and, like the absurdity at the heart of that tragedy, he kept brushing the foam off with one hand and shaking his fist at Goddard. It was as if he did not know which was worse, being deprived of his beer ration or looking like someone in a comic movie.

Belowdecks, Lorimer's guards had recovered themselves and now took him "by the scruff of the neck" back up through the darkened ship to the quarterdeck, where "all hell was reigning," Lorimer remembered. "Sailors were rushing about; there was a lot of fist shaking at us, and all the small guns seemed to be firing. The sea was absolutely calm and at the slightest ripple every gun they could bring to bear on it was loosed off."

Cameron, too, was up on deck by then, and as all four of them were lined against a bulkhead opposite the same eight men with Tommy guns, they were convinced that they were now facing a firing squad. The officer in charge kept waving his pistol at them and shouting, "How many? How many?" Whether he meant how many more submarines had come to attack the ship or how many more bombs were set to go off they did not know. When they would not answer, he turned and shouted at the eight men with Tommy guns, telling them to keep their eyes on the prisoners, that there might be more explosions, and that if the prisoners tried to escape they were to be shot.

The British, understanding none of this, were convinced that they were doomed, until a high-ranking officer came aboard up the gangway astern. It was Admiral Oskar Kummetz, and, as if symbolizing the German Navy Command's belief in the absolute safety of Kaafjord, he was wearing riding breeches and boots and carrying a crop. He had been out for his morning ride, and the explosion had sent him galloping back to see what had happened. On his way to the bridge, he stopped when he saw the four bearded prisoners and spoke for a moment or two to the officer in charge. When he left, the officer put his pistol away, giving the prisoners the mistaken impression that Kummetz had countermanded the order to shoot them.

"I didn't know the admiral's name," Lorimer said later, "but under my breath I thanked him."

Lorimer was as bitterly disappointed as his comrades were

to see the *Tirpitz* still afloat. They had no reason to be. If they had been able to see what had happened below the water line, they would have realized how seriously, in fact how irreparably, they had crippled the ship.

All the lower decks were flooded, and in the turbine rooms midship the inrushing water was mixing with the fuel and motor oil. The ship's drinking water was salted, part of her food supply contaminated, her portholes shattered, and her crockery and glassware smashed. All the pipe connections along the bottom of the ship were broken and the machinery's fundamental bolts and casings torn from their moorings; the bilge pumps were knocked out, and the cables for the various switches torn from their channels. Engineers and oilers had to use wooden hammer handles to push the loose and hanging cables back in place to avoid being electrocuted.

There were two sections of diesel generators, one on the port side and one on the starboard, each with four engines. The explosion near the stern had completely flooded the port section and knocked out all four engines. In the unflooded starboard section it had knocked out three. With the whole ship operating on only one diesel generator, the engine room, on orders from the bridge, started to give power to the ship selectively. Power to pump water out of the flooded compartments came first. Battle readiness, the communication system, and a minimum of illumination below decks came next, in that order of importance. But everything else—galleys, bakery, heating—was cut off.

Because of this electrical breakdown, it was impossible to ignite any boiler to produce steam. The burner blocks in the aft boiler rooms were too damaged to ignite anyway, but those in the forward boiler room were undamaged, and had it not been for the sixteen-minute delay in ordering steam in the first place, they might have been ignited before the explosion.

"The order was to fire the boilers," Engineer Walter Stube, in charge of the ship's boilers, said later. "But since there was no electricity, the order was impossible to carry out. We tried tapping the diesel-oil pipe and spraying the oil into the boiler

Sub-Lieutenant (now Rear Admiral) B. C. Godfrey Place, RN, captain of the X-7

Lieutenant Donald Cameron, RNR, captain of British midget submarine X-6

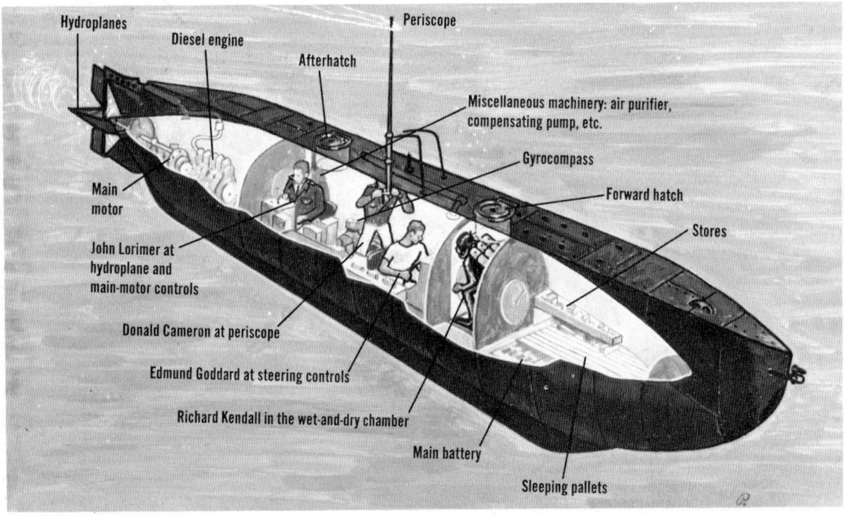

Hydroplanes
Diesel engine
Periscope
Afterhatch
Miscellaneous machinery: air purifier, compensating pump, etc.
Gyrocompass
Forward hatch
Stores
Main motor
John Lorimer at hydroplane and main-motor controls
Donald Cameron at periscope
Edmund Goddard at steering controls
Richard Kendall in the wet-and-dry chamber
Main battery
Sleeping pallets

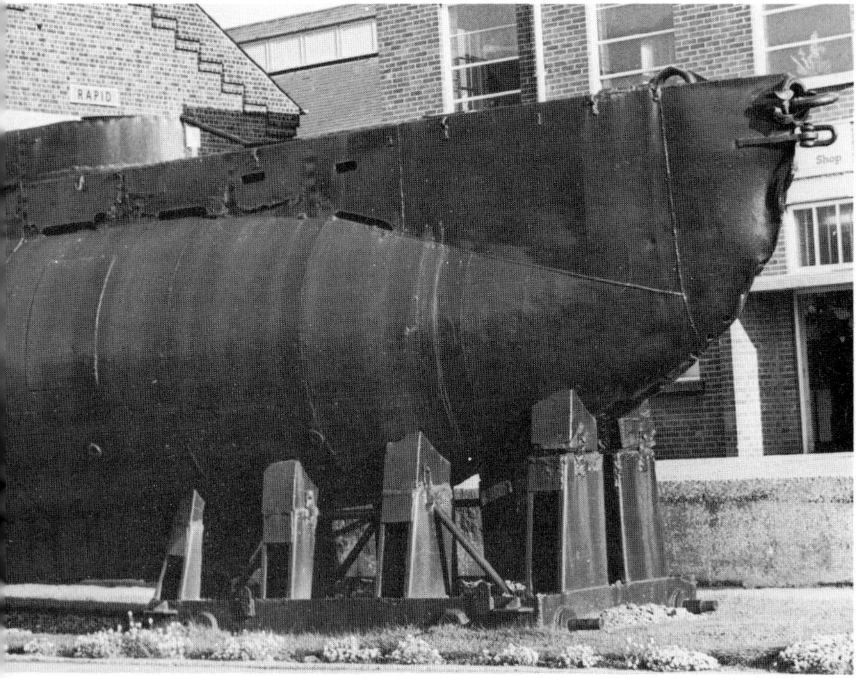

The only surviving British midget submarine, now on display at H.M.S. *Dolphin,* the Royal Navy's submarine base at Portsmouth, England. The side charge extends from bow to stern. [Ministry of Defence (Navy). Copyright reserved]

The interior of the X-6, showing the crew at work
[Copyright © 1969 The Reader's Digest Association]

Periscope in the X-craft. [Ministry of Defence (Navy) Copyright reserved]

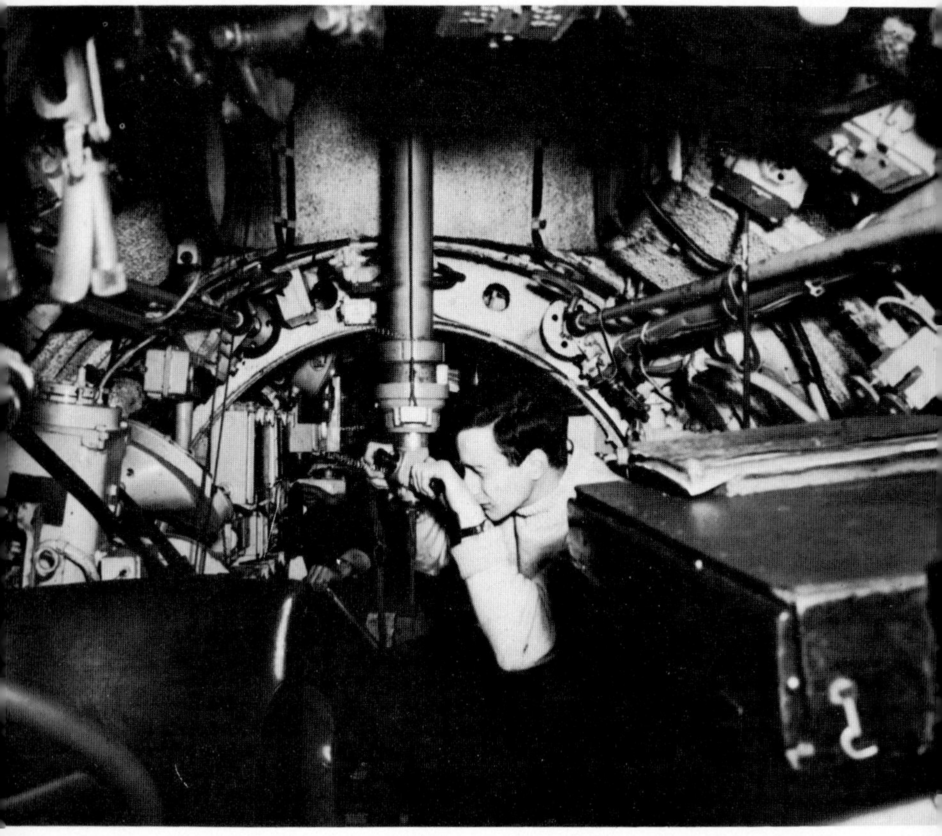

Steering controls of the X-craft. [Ministry of Defence (Navy) Copyright reserved]

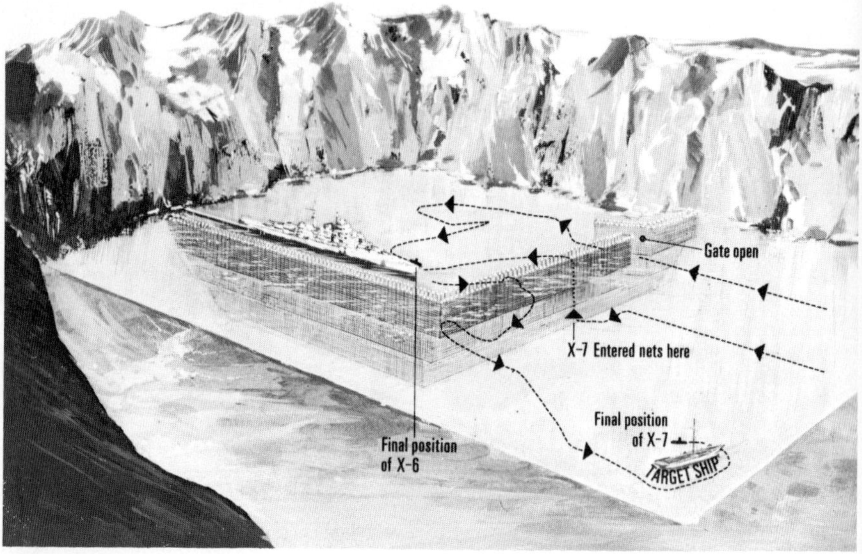

The *Tirpitz* in her Kaafjord berth and the routes of the midget submarines X-6 and X-7 in their attack on her [Copyright © 1970 The Reader's Digest Association]

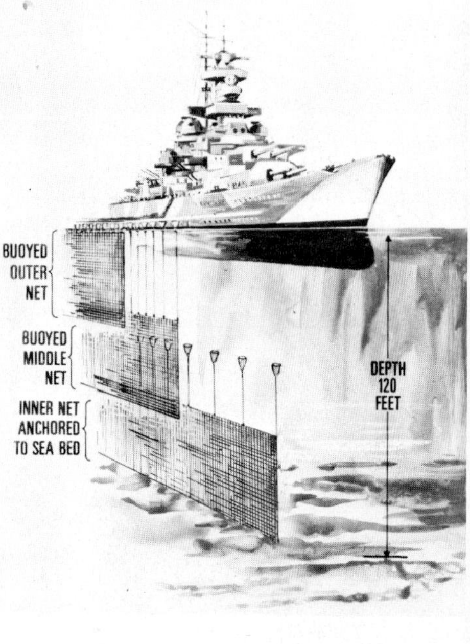

Cross-section showing the antitorpedo net protecting the *Tirpitz* in Kaafjord [Copyright © 1970 The Reader's Digest Association]

Specifications of the *Tirpitz*

DISPLACEMENT: actual, 56,000 tons; nominal, 42,900 tons
LENGTH: over-all, 828 feet; at water line, 798 feet
BEAM: 119 feet DRAFT: 32 to 37 feet
ENGINES: 3 groups of turbines of 48,000 horsepower each; 12 boilers with water tubes of 55 atmospheres each of 58 kilograms—475° C
SPEED: maximum, 30.8 knots; normal, 28 knots
ENDURANCE: 9,000 miles at 19 knots
OIL FUEL: 8,700 tons PROPELLERS: 3
ELECTRICAL INSTALLATION: 2 turbo-electric generators; 2 diesel generators of 2,000 kilowatts each
ARMAMENT: main, 4 twin turrets, 8 15″ guns; secondary, 6 twin turrets, 12 5.9″ guns; 8 twin mountings, 16 4.1″ guns; antiaircraft, 8 twin 37-mm. mountings, 16 quadruple 20-mm. mountings
TORPEDOES: 2 quadruple 21″ mountings
AIRCRAFT: 4 seaplanes, Type 196, launched by catapult
SHIP'S COMPANY: 2,340 (60 officers, 80 warrant officers, 500 petty officers and leading ratings, 1,700 ratings)

Earlier photograph of the *Tirpitz* in Kaafjord taken by an RAF reconnaissance plane [NTB]

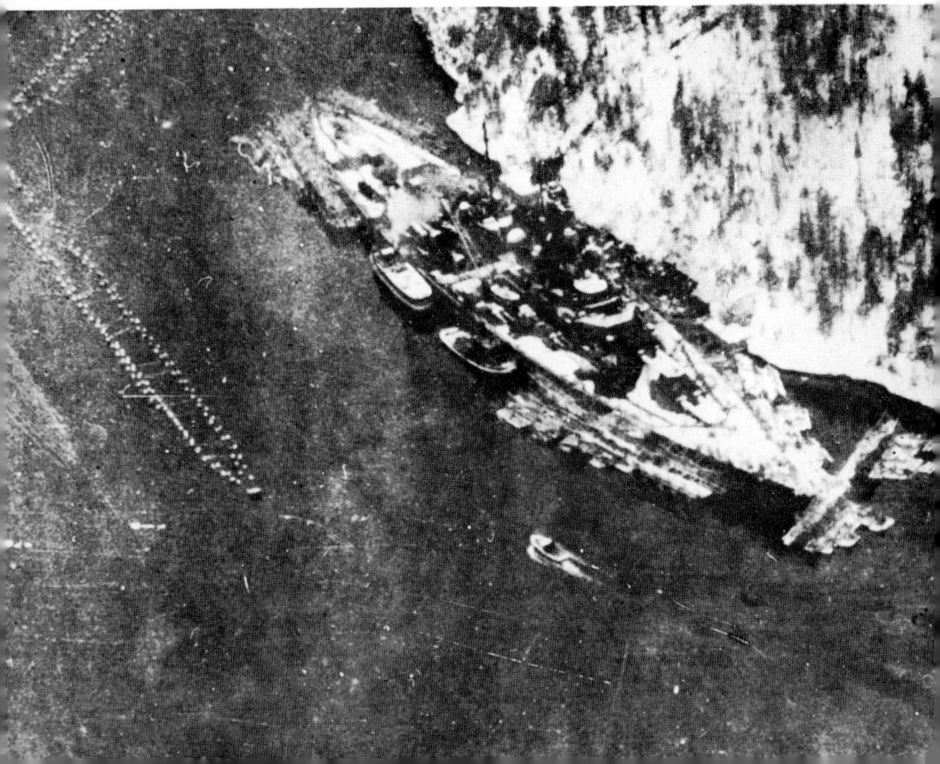

Harry Pettersen, of the Norwegian Resistance, who supplied information on the *Tirpitz* to the British, and John Lorimer, of the X-6 crew, revisiting in 1967 the *Tirpitz* anchorage in Kaafjord, Norway

Crest designed for the X-craft [Ministry of Defence (Navy). Copyright reserved]

by hand, but all the huge ventilators had broken and were unable to bring air into the boiler rooms, so even igniting the undamaged burner blocks was going to be much slower."

"After the explosion the ship could not be moved," Chief Engineer Eichler said. "There was so much out of order and so much checking to do, that for all intents and purposes the ship was helpless."

The aft fifteen-inch-gun turret, weighing 30,000 pounds, was lifted by the explosion and thrown completely out of line. The electrical range finders and the gunnery control circuits were out of order. In fact, if the British had attacked by air after the explosion, the ship would have been almost without the means to protect herself. Except for a few of her lighter, hand-operated guns, the antiaircraft batteries in the hills, and the fjord's smoke-screen apparatus, she would have been at the mercy of a carrier-based air attack. With only one generator operating, there would have been insufficient electricity to operate the ammunition elevators and turrets and still keep the pumps going to empty the ship of water.

A follow-up air attack was indeed what the German crew feared most. Even if the British had planned one, however, they would not have carried it out, for they already knew that four of their midget-submarine crewmen had been captured and taken aboard the *Tirpitz.* All around Kaafjord, Norwegians had gathered to watch from the moment *Tirpitz* gunners started shooting rifles and throwing grenades at X-6. Many were in the general store on the east side of the fjord when the firing started. They saw the crew of X-6 captured and the ship being hurled upward by the explosion.

"I was standing by the general store watching the whole thing," Harry Pettersen's father said later. "Other home owners and fishermen were there, too. We knew the ship was badly damaged because the stern was resting on the bottom. It wasn't very noticeable because the water there isn't very deep. We knew there had to be a hole in the bottom for the stern to be down that way, though, and we were all happy about it. . . . Then German soldiers came and chased us away."

With Harry Pettersen's father an eyewitness, it did not take long for a great deal of pertinent information to be passed on to Rasmussen and Raaby, who passed it on to London.

Meanwhile, the four prisoners on the quarterdeck were wondering what had happened to the X-craft they had seen slipping over the nets off the starboard bow. Had she escaped or was she still hiding somewhere at the bottom of Kaafjord? Then to their amazement, and everyone else's, a midget submarine suddenly surfaced in almost exactly the same place as seen before—off the starboard bow just outside the net cage. It was X-7, blown free of the nets by the explosion.

"On surfacing it was tiresome to see the *Tirpitz* still afloat," Godfrey Place said later, in his charmingly understated way. "This made me uncertain as to whether the explosion we had just heard was our own charges or depth charges, so X-7 was taken to the bottom to survey the damage."

Compasses and diving gauges were out of order, though there appeared to be little structural damage. Place decided to try to escape just under the surface, at periscope depth, but when they went up again, the craft was impossible to control and broke surface several times. Now over a hundred yards from the net cage, she was fired on each time, until finally her hull was hit by small shells and bullets from the ship's secondary armament and machine guns.

"Dive!" Place ordered.

Down at 125 feet they felt themselves getting wet. A jet of water was spurting into the midget, and water was trickling down the hull from between the plates. Bob Aitken grabbed his tool case, got tow, and began stopping up the cracks, but they all realized that escape was out of the question now.

They decided to open the sea cocks, wait until the craft filled with water, and save themselves with their Davis escape apparatus. Once X-7 was completely flooded, they could leave two at a time, one through the control-room hatch and one through the wet-and-dry chamber.

But when depth charges began exploding all around them,

they had to abandon this method of escape. On their way up they would all have been crushed by the water pressure created by the depth charges.

"We'll surface and abandon ship," Place said. "Bring her to full buoyancy."

He left the periscope and went toward the hatch, under which Bill Whittam, his first officer, was sitting. Whittam got up to let him stand on the seat to unscrew the hatch cover. The hail of bullets that had greeted their previous surfacings had brought Place to a decision that even today must haunt him. Instead of abandoning ship last, in accordance with the tradition of the sea, he would abandon her first, in order to expose himself, and not his men, to the small-arms fire. The Germans might kill the first man out of the hatch, but once they saw that the craft was being abandoned, they would surely hold their fire.

At 0835 the craft surfaced, close to a moored gunnery target. Immediately Place gave the order to abandon ship, threw the hatch open to a blaze of sunlight and a rush of fresh air, and began climbing out. The battered craft was rolling, and above the noise of a rain of bullets, and with water pouring down around him into the control room, he cried, "Here goes the last of the Places!"

Holding up his thick white sweater to indicate surrender, he managed to tumble onto the casing and into the sea without being hit. He swam, boots and all, his sweater in his teeth, to the gunnery target. Climbing up on it, he looked back to see if his men were following him as planned and was shocked and dismayed to see only water behind him. Though the firing had stopped, as he had hoped, the floundering craft had gone down before the others could escape. Had they closed the hatch in time? Were they preparing the Davis escape apparatus for their ascent from the bottom? Surely the Germans would stop dropping depth charges now.

While he was pondering these things, with his freezing and wet long underwear clinging to him, a German picket boat came to pick him up. He wrung out his sweater and put it on.

When he reached the quarterdeck of the *Tirpitz,* he was greeted with great fondness by Cameron and his men.

"Godfrey was wearing an enormous pair of boots, a submarine sweater, and long submarine issue pants, with no trousers," Lorimer recalled. "He was a cheering sight, standing there shivering underneath the guns of Y turret." The boots were those he had borrowed from Peter Philip three days earlier.

But as happy as Lorimer was to see Place alive and well, and as confident as he was that the others in X-7 would soon be using their Davis escape apparatus to reach the surface, he could not take his mind off what he had just seen far out on the water. Another midget had surfaced and dived again about five hundred yards abeam. It had to be Henty-Creer's X-5. He had been watching her periscope for over a minute, wondering why she did not dive and run. With the firing period still not over, she had no business being anywhere near the ship. Since she was outside the net cage, in open water, she could not be caught up on anything. Get under, he kept thinking, run!

It may be that X-5, like X-7, had been battered by the explosion and had to be abandoned. Through his periscope Henty-Creer might have seen X-7 surface and Place jump into the sea. His intention might have been similar: he would surface and they would abandon the craft.

But the truth will never be known. When, at 0843, X-5 surfaced the second time, in full view of the five prisoners on deck, she was blasted out of the water before her hatch could be opened. Unlike X-6 and X-7, she had surfaced within the angle of depression of the battleship's four-inch guns, and at five hundred yards she had no chance. She and her crew of four went down in very deep water, into cold, rock-ribbed chasms too deep for divers to reach. To this day she has not been recovered.

After watching her disappear, Place turned painfully toward the water off the starboard bow. Had the three men he had left behind in X-7 closed the hatch in time? Were they at the bottom preparing their escape?

19

From the moment Place had jumped from X-7 into the sea, the craft, with her battered hull leaking and water rushing into the control room through the open hatch, had taken on a severe list to starboard and started downward.

"We're sinking," shouted Whittam.

Fighting his way onto the seat against the massive downpour of water, he reached up, grabbed the hatch cover and just managed to close and screw it. They were only about six feet beneath the surface. For the next few seconds every effort was directed toward reaching the surface again. But the craft was pitching and rolling; her cracked ballast tanks could not be vented. She was sinking deeper and deeper, and there was nothing they could do about it. Gripping pipes and cables to hold their balance, they stared at one another, silent and motionless, their eyes and expressions and even their postures showing alarm and consternation. Nor was there any need for words. The craft was going down for the last time, and they were waiting for her to come to rest before taking further action. When she stopped pitching and rolling, they remained as they were, staring stonelike at one another. Then, as though in slow motion, there was a slight bump, a slow, almost lazy rebound, and another bump as the craft came silently to rest in 120 feet of water.

"Get out the Davis escape apparatus," Whittam said, taking charge at once now that Place was gone.

Aitken, X-7's huge diver, got them from the storage locker and helped Whittam and Willie Whitley put theirs on. Then he went to the battery compartment for his diving suit and began struggling into it: rubber tunic, waist-high rubber boots with leaded soles, lead-weighted belt, rubber gloves, and, strapped to the small of his back, oxygen cylinders connected by flexible rubber tubing to a rubber face mask that he would slip on later.

"We were all pretty calm," he reported later, although, being a highly trained diver with experience at much greater depths, he was by far the calmest. "The pressure at 120 feet was nothing after the training I had had under Commander Chadwick at Portsmouth."

Whittam and Whitley, though, were not trained divers. They had been taught how to use the Davis escape apparatus in the indoor diving tank at Portsmouth, but that had been in almost tepid water at less than one third this depth.

"We're between 120 and 130 feet down," Whittam said. "What do you think, Bob? You're the expert. What are our chances?"

With no more depth charges falling, they could hear the water seeping through the hull's fractured frames. Instinctively they glanced down, but it had not reached the deck boards yet.

"Should we take turns escaping from the wet-and-dry chamber?" Whittam went on.

Aitken thought about it in silence for a moment. With so much already out of order in the craft, the valves controlling the flow of water between the main ballast tank and the wet-and-dry chamber might not function as they should. Besides, at this depth it would take each man at least thirty minutes to flood the chamber to prevent too rapid a build-up of pressure on his body. The first man might make it, and maybe the second. But with water constantly seeping into the craft, the controls might be shorted before the third man got his turn. Worse still, the first man out would have to close the hatch behind him before ascending to the surface. Otherwise the second man would have no way of emptying the chamber of water before climbing in himself. Then the second man would have to do the same thing for the third man.

If Whittam and Whitley had been experienced divers, or if they at least had had the kind of diving suit, with weighted belt and boots, that he had, they might have been able to hang on to the craft long enough to close the hatch before ascending. But Aitken knew from experience that once the pressure inside an escape chamber equalizes, and the man inside is able to open the hatch, he experiences an almost overwhelming urge to get to the surface just as fast as the buoyancy of his body will take him. Even experienced divers find it hard to resist this urge, especially in panic situations, though they, of all people, know what irreparable damage the body can suffer from too rapid an ascent from deep beneath the surface.

"No. I think we should flood the craft and use both hatches at the same time," Aitken said. "Willie can go by the one here in the control room, and you, Bill, can go by the one forward in the wet-and-dry. I'll use whichever one is clear first."

Whittam agreed and immediately ordered the sea cocks opened to accelerate the inflow of water.

"Now let's have a recap," Aitken said. "At this depth the pressure in here is going to increase until it equals the pressure of about five atmospheres, or roughly seventy pounds to the square inch. We'll have to work up to that pressure gradually, by adjusting our distributors as more and more water comes in."

The water was by now beginning to cover the deck boards. They were standing in it; their shoes were getting wet.

"When do we start?" Whitley asked.

"Not yet. Not until the water reaches the batteries and starts generating gas," Aitken said. "There's just so much oxygen in these tanks, so the more we save now, the more we'll have later."

"How long do they last?"

"At this pressure, about forty-five minutes. Then there's the smaller cylinder. If your main cylinder runs out, turn on the small one, and you'll get four or five more minutes. If the small one runs out, the two oxylets attached to your equipment will give you a few more breaths—just in case you need them on your way up to the surface."

When the water covered their ankles, the anxiety and suspense of waiting prompted them to run through their escape procedure: Whittam through the wet-and-dry chamber up forward, Whitley through the control-room hatch aft, and Aitken through whichever one was clear first. But with Aitken in his diving suit and Whittam and Whitley wearing their escape apparatus, they found they could not get past one another. No matter how hard Aitken tried to get between them to the middle of the control room, so that Whittam would be forward of him and Whitley aft of him, he found himself short by several inches.

It was one of those unforeseen, even ridiculous mishaps that at any other time would have caused derisive laughter, for despite all the time, thought, preparation, and foresight that had gone into the mission, no one had thought of checking to see whether a crew fully equipped with escape apparatus, with the diver in his diving suit, could maneuver inside a midget submarine. Even with Place gone and only three of them left, they were locked in the same positions they had been in when they had donned their equipment. Aitken would have to remove his diving suit, let Whittam pass forward of him, and then put his suit on again—an exhausting chore even under the most favorable conditions—or their escape procedure would have to be changed.

"All right," Whittam said. "When the craft fills, Bob, you'll go out first by the wet-and-dry, since you're closest to it. Then when you get out, stay there, just outside the craft, and help us through whichever hatch we get to first. That way, we can all go up together."

All this time the water had been rising, but not nearly fast enough. It was reaching their knees and, fed as it was by recent snows and endless glacial drainage from the surrounding mountainsides, it felt as cold and hard as ice. They tried to open three other vents, but could not because the battering the hull had suffered had thrown everything out of line. There was nothing to do but wait. In an effort to postpone standing in the rising water for as long as possible, Whittam and Whitley stood on seats, with their backs bent around the inner curvature of the hull.

It was an uncomfortable position to maintain for any length of time, but, more important, it was a repugnant one as well. Even men who know they are doomed care about how they appear to themselves and others, and standing there like that, bent over on chairs waiting for the water to reach them, made them feel foolish at a time when they had every right and reason to feel important. And the forced change in the escape procedure had started a subtle poison coursing through them. They were losing their confidence little by little, thinking of the diminishing air in the craft, of the time when they would have water up to their mouths, their eyes, over their heads.

In an effort to encourage them, Aitken recalled the escape of Lorimer, Gay, and Laites from X-3 in Loch Striven.

"They were down at about the same depth," he said, "but Lorimer got them out with the same escape apparatus we're using."

"You're right," Whittam said, turning toward Aitken with his neck between two projecting pipes. "It was in November of last year. We're in precisely the same position now, so all we have to do is wait and do as they did."

They were not in precisely the same position, and they knew it, but they refrained from saying so. The water in Loch Striven at the time of Lorimer's escape had been almost sixty degrees warmer than the water here in Kaafjord, which was not merely cold, but literally, with its salt content, close to the zero-degree level. They knew how rapidly a man burns oxygen when exposed to such water; they had panted under too many cold showers during training not to know. But there was no need to discuss it; the knowledge was there in the control room with them just as surely as the rising water was.

After a short silence, Aitken brought up other successful escapes, detailing the differences and similarities between their situation and all the others he had known or heard about, in both England and America, in small and large submarines. Without realizing it he was trying to relate what was happening to them to something habitual, in the past, that their imaginations might at least pursue. It was a splendid attempt, and it helped; it was better than nothing, better than silence. But what they needed most was something to *do* while waiting, something urgent and all-consuming enough to come between them and their growing anxiety. There was nothing to do, though, nothing at all, so they waited—for half an hour, forty minutes.

The water had risen high enough over the seats to cover Whittam's and Whitley's shoes and ankles. Their feet and then, gradually, their ankles and calves began to pain them as the deadly cold chased the blood away. If they could have rigged some high-slung hammock to the ceiling and climbed into it, or done anything else to postpone exposing themselves to the freezing water, they would have. But there was nothing to be done, and their backs were breaking.

"Well, here goes," Whittam said uncertainly.

There was something poignantly reminiscent of peacetime in his tone and expression. Like a bather at the beach who knows the water is cold but who nevertheless cannot help expressing surprise at how really cold it is the moment he gets wet, he stepped down from the seat onto the deck boards and stood there, thigh-deep in it, making involuntary sounds, movements, and expressions of astonishment.

When Whitley followed, looking like a man on stilts in his effort to keep as much of his body out of it as possible, Aitken's heart ached for them. "Don't move around unless you have to," he said. "Your feet and legs will warm the water in your shoes and trousers, so try not to disturb that water. Let it stay there."

He had not finished speaking when the water reached an electric circuit and caused the fuse wires to explode. An acrid smoke filled the control room. Then the lights went out, and from the battery compartment forward there came a hissing sound. All three knew what that meant. The water had reached the batteries and was mixing with the battery acids.

As quietly and calmly as possible, Aitken said, "From now on we'll have to use our escape oxygen."

He knew that any unnecessary excitement in his voice would only generate more excitement, especially now that all the lights were out. It took only a second or two, in fact, for the darkness to exaggerate everything—the hissing sound, the sound of water seeping in, even the slightest sloshing movement any one of them made in the rising water. If by some miracle the lights had gone on again, each man would have been shocked by the sight of the other two, for the darkness had already separated them, robbed them of their earlier reluctance to express in their eyes and faces the true horror of the situation. The stabilizing influence of seeing and being seen was gone, and now, with their rubber mouthpieces in their mouths, so was the ability to communicate by speech.

"It was utter darkness," Aitken said later, "a coffin. The two others were standing near me. There was nothing to be done. The water, or ice, rather, kept rising, but we could still only wait."

From time to time they turned the knobs on their distributors to adjust the pressure to the increasing pressure inside the craft. The hissing sound had stopped and so had the sound of seeping water. The only sounds now would be made by them, by one man adjusting his distributor, another shuddering from cold or fear, another reaching out to encourage and be encouraged. Never in their lives had sound—the slightest, most insignificant sound—been more important. It kept them listening, kept them alive.

"The water was up to our chests," Aitken recalled. "Its icy grip was like a vise. By then the craft was near enough flooded, so I went into the wet-and-dry and tried to open the hatch."

The pressure had still not equalized, though, and even using all his strength he was unable to move it. He would just have to wait a while and then try again. But there were only minutes left. His main oxygen cylinder was almost empty, which meant that Whittam's and Whitley's probably *were* empty. If they had already started on their emergency supply . . .

Tapping his reserve cylinder, he climbed as quickly as possible through the opening into the control room and made his way aft to where he had left Whitley, propped up against the periscope. He was worried in particular about Whitley, who had appeared uncertain earlier as to how to adjust his distributor—not that Whittam had been very sure of himself either. On the other hand, they might already have started working on the other hatch. If so, and they succeeded in opening it, they could all escape through it.

Feeling his way through the water and darkness as he went, he was surprised, puzzled, and finally confused when his hand met a void. Whitley was gone. But where? For just a second, he thought he might be losing his mind. Then his foot knocked against something soft. Whitley had fallen and was lying across the deck boards.

"I leaned over and put my hand on his face, his chest, his oxygen bottle. The breathing bag was empty, flat, completely flat; the two emergency oxylets were empty, too. Poor old Whitley couldn't be still alive, and even if he was, I couldn't hope to lift him, get him out and bring him to the surface. . . ."

Reaching over Whitley's body at about knee level to see if Whittam was still alive, he almost blacked out as the oxygen in his reserve cylinder began to run out. Realizing he had only enough left for a few seconds, he quickly opened his two emergency oxylets. But at that depth they seemed to give him no more than a breath apiece.

"Whittam was almost certainly dead, too," he said. "So there I was in a flooded submarine with two dead men at 120 feet, my last oxygen reserves gone, and nothing left but the breath in my lungs."

He remembered scrambling back into the escape chamber "for one more go at the hatch." Then things went black; he fainted and fell over on the toilet seat. He was only alive enough now to make death possible, and yet the endeavor to persist in his own being expressed itself in the way his hands and arms kept reaching up for the hatch as though he were still telling them to. His last wish and desire had been to open the hatch and escape, but he had no recollection of opening it. Somehow, though, he did open it, and when his eyes opened he saw a stream of bubbles all around him as he sped to the surface. The cold air and the sun revived him. At last, after more than two hours down at the bottom of Kaafjord, he saw the sky.

A German surface craft spotted him immediately, and in a few minutes he was brought aboard the *Tirpitz*, a haggard man with death still in his eyes but with life in his pounding heart.

Aftermath

20

That afternoon all six British prisoners were given schnapps on orders from Captain Hans Meyer, who had earlier watched them with admiration from the bridge but who was too reserved and shy to meet and question them. They were then taken below, where the lights had been partially restored, and locked in single, blacked-out cells.

"On my way down," Lorimer said later, "I realized how much interior damage the explosion had caused. The fire damage control was all broken, as were water and fuel pipes. The decks were in a state of shambles, but as the *Tirpitz* was lifted some seven feet out of the water by the explosion, perhaps this was not surprising. . . .

"I was pushed into my cell, and the door slammed shut. The only furniture was a wooden bunk, which was lying in a heap on the floor, presumably as a result of the explosion. At first there was no light, but after a couple of hours a German rating came along and replaced the bulb. . . . The cell was about ten by eight feet, and apart from a small grill in the middle of the door, it was a small steel box."

A Norwegian taken prisoner during the Spitsbergen raid two weeks earlier had occupied the same cell, and as Lorimer recalled, "The otherwise bare painted walls were covered with the most disrespectful drawings of Hitler, each with an appropriate comment written underneath."

Later that afternoon he was taken up to another cabin for further interrogation, this time by an official German interpreter who had been specially flown up from Tromsö. "This man's English was very good," Lorimer said. "He was under the impression that we were commandos, and I did not disillusion him. The Germans at that time seemed to be very afraid of the commandos, and from then on until we reached Germany we had about six guards each whenever we were moved from one place to another. On my return to my cell I was given some coffee and cold meat, which I was very glad to get. I did not sleep much that night, thinking about what a mess we had landed ourselves in and wondering about our people at home."

Shortly before leaving on the mission, Lorimer had become engaged to Judith Hughes-Onslow, a bright, trim, vivacious, and charming Wren in the Signals Division. Having seen the midget submarines on the surface in Loch Striven, Miss Hughes-Onslow knew they existed, and having handled highly sensitive messages in Signals, she knew they were going on a secret mission. But Lorimer had told her nothing about them or for what they were intended, and now, locked in his cell, he could only hope that the *Times* would say nothing about the attack rather than something that would almost certainly have to be, for security reasons, only partially true.

As it happened, his fears were justified. The *Times* reported that the *Tirpitz* had been attacked by British midget submarines and that all the submariners were missing and presumed killed. Among others, Judith Hughes-Onslow, Eve Cameron, and Althea Place, the delightful Wren Godfrey Place had married only weeks before leaving on the mission, had to wait months to learn that the men were still alive.

After spending only one night in cells aboard the *Tirpitz,* the prisoners, with Captain Meyer watching from a distance, were escorted from the ship by armed guards and put aboard a German motor torpedo boat. Looking back for the last time at the *Tirpitz* as they passed through the mouth of Kaafjord, they were all bitterly disappointed that she was still afloat. Despite the damage done to her, in their eyes the mission had been a failure.

They were taken first to Tromsö, where they spent the night in a German barracks. The following morning they were put aboard a mine sweeper and taken farther south, through Ofotfjord, to Narvik. Here they created a problem. There was no building secure enough for the safe custody of "commandos," who would know that Sweden and freedom were only fifteen miles away. The Germans, fearing an escape attempt, took over a school building, wired all the windows, set up bunks for the prisoners in one of the classrooms, and for the next two days surrounded the building with thirty armed guards.

"In Narvik we were interviewed by a very nice old German commander who gave us each a comb, toothbrush, and toothpaste," Lorimer remembered. "He told us that he personally would get in touch with the International Red Cross so that our relatives would be informed that we were safe and well. I think that he genuinely meant to do this but was not allowed to, as the first indication any of our relatives had that we were in fact prisoners was our first letters, which they did not receive until February of the following year, five months later."

After their stay in Narvik, they were once again put aboard a mine sweeper, and were taken to Trondheim and locked up in an ancient and wet dungeon on an island in the harbor. "These quarters were most unpleasant," Lorimer said, "but in spite of our vigorous complaints and invocation of the Geneva Convention regarding the treatment of prisoners of war, we remained there for three days before being put on a train for Oslo.

"From Oslo we went by ferry to Aarhus, in Denmark, and then by train to Dulag Nord, the naval interrogation camp between Bremen and Hamburg. It had taken us three weeks to get from Kaafjord to Germany. Whilst in the care of the German Navy, particularly the mine sweepers, we received every courtesy and we were well fed and given beer and cigarettes, each of us being locked up in one of the officers' cabins."

At Dulag Nord they were subjected to forty-five days of solitary confinement, interrogation, and an irreducible minimum of food. The German officers doing the questioning were both accomplished linguists and experts at putting a man off guard. Just as Lorimer had anticipated, they finally produced the two photographs of Norwegian patriots that had been slipped in among his belongings aboard the *Tirpitz.* United States Secretary of the Navy Frank Knox had announced in Washington on October 12, 1943, that the *Tirpitz* had been attacked by British midget submarines with two-men crews, and the Germans could not understand why X-6 had had a four-man crew when X-7 had presumably had only a two-man crew, consisting of Godfrey Place and Robert Aitken.

When they confronted Lorimer with the photographs and accused him of being a secret agent, and so subject to execution, he stood up, took the photographs, and successfully pleaded his innocence by showing the Germans that the photographs were simply too large to have fit in his pockets. He would have had to fold them to do so, and they had quite obviously not been folded. He was therefore not a secret agent.

From their solitary confinement at Dulag Nord they were taken, on November 28, to Marlag-Milag Nord, in northern Germany, a camp for Navy personnel. There they were treated quite well. Indeed, as the war continued, and the probability of Germany's defeat increased, they were treated better and better.

"Apart from being bloody hungry most of the time," Lorimer said, "our stay at Marlag-Milag Nord was amusing and interesting. Only 350 naval officers were captured during the entire war, and as Navy men were gentlemen in the eyes of the Germans, we were treated accordingly. Don Cameron was even able to finagle a drawing pad and put his talents as an artist to use—by doing caricatures of the jailers."

They spent the remainder of the war at Marlag-Milag Nord, talking about their mission against the *Tirpitz,* second-guessing themselves, regretting what they considered to be its failure after all the concentration, effort, and dedication they had put into it.

They had no reason for regrets. Two days after their attack, when Admiral Doenitz flew to Kaafjord, read the damage reports, and made a thorough check of the ship himself, he issued a prophetic statement.

"One thing is certain," he said. "If the *Tirpitz* puts to sea after this, it can only be on her death ride."

With Hitler's approval and the concurrence of Admiral Kummetz and Captain Meyer, he decided not to attempt to move the ship to Germany for repairs. For one thing, it was hoped that since none of the damage was visible from the outside, the British would not know for sure that the ship had been put out of action, and, for another, certain hull frames had been fractured, raising doubts about the ship's ability to steam at high speed ever again. The huge hole in her bottom could be sealed, but with her rudder severely damaged, she would have to be towed to Germany at too slow a speed not to invite what would undoubtedly be a fatal attack.

Of course the British Admiralty knew much more about the damage than the Germans realized, for every day, as more information was gathered by Norwegians supplying the ship with provisions, it was passed on to Rasmussen and Pettersen and then wired to London by Raaby.

Meanwhile, over 1,000 shipworkers in Hamburg had boarded a specially chartered ship of the Hamburg-Südamerike Line, the *Monte Rosa,* and were on their way to the north of Norway to try to repair the *Tirpitz* and make her operational again. It was a long, dangerous voyage, and while waiting for them to arrive, Captain Meyer ordered a search for the sunken midget submarines. X-5 had gone down in water far too deep for her ever to be reached, and X-6 had been destroyed by the explosion of her own side charges. But X-7 was salvageable, because she had gone down off the ship's starboard bow, where the water was deep but not beyond the reach of divers.

"We dragged hooks along the bottom of the fjord and got our divers down," Meyer said later. "Eventually, after several days, lots of work and many attempts, we found Godfrey Place's midget at a depth of forty-four meters and brought it ashore. There were two dead sailors in the boat. . . ."

Whittam and Whitley, the two men whose lives Aitken had tried in vain to save, were reportedly buried on land with military honors, but there were no Norwegian witnesses to the burial, and to this day no graves, marked or otherwise, have been found.

Although the whole of X-7's bow was missing, having been blown off by one of the depth charges dropped following Aitken's escape, the craft contained many maps, photographs, and documents that intrigued the Germans. Kummetz, for one, was surprised at how well informed the British Admiralty had been about the many details of life aboard the *Tirpitz.*

"From the material found in the salvaged midget," he wrote in a top-secret German Naval War Staff report, "it can be deduced that the attack was very well organized and prepared."

One of the captured documents was an accurate service roster, showing the routine of duties on board the *Tirpitz* for the week of September 21. The British had deliberately chosen the day of weapon-cleaning, when they could expect a lot of shipboard noise and a less vigilant watch, for their attack. To the dismay of Kummetz, who had looked upon the *Tirpitz* as being untouchable in Kaafjord, the British even knew that the sound-detection equipment was to be overhauled that day.

Every changing of the guard—at the boat-gate entrance to Kaafjord, the boat gate in the antitorpedo nets around the ship, and at all the gangway stations—was also known to the British. There were remarkable relief maps of the *Tirpitz*'s anchorage in Kaafjord, diagrams showing a surprising knowledge of the internal structure of the ship, and several photographs of her, taken from ahead, at an angle, and from both sides.

Whether it was because of these captured documents, which supplied ample proof of the excellent contact between the Norwegian Resistance and the British, or because the Germans were overreacting to a humiliating and costly defeat, the Gestapo redoubled its efforts in the north of Norway following the X-craft attack. Unfortunately, because of the carelessness of one Resistance agent in Tromsö, who was caught with a book containing names, Karl Rasmussen was arrested and taken to Gestapo headquarters in Tromsö. It was a four-story stone building, and in a small, sparsely furnished room on the fourth floor, he was questioned, tortured, and questioned again. After all his nails had been ripped off, he jumped headlong through the window, killing himself, as he had always vowed he would if he ever came close to betraying Raaby and Pettersen. Because he chose his own death over betrayal of his friends, he is remembered with great admiration and warmth by Harry Pettersen, who still lives on the shore of Kaafjord, less than a hundred yards from where the *Tirpitz* once so largely loomed. Torstein Raaby, an inveterate adventurer long after taking part in the *Kon Tiki* voyage in 1947, died of heart failure on his way to the North Pole in 1964.

When the *Monte Rosa* arrived in Kaafjord with the 1,000 shipyard workers and the repair ship *Neumark,* of the Wilhelmshaven naval yard, work began on resetting the ship's turbines in their mountings, replacing the broken pipelines, splicing the torn electrical cables, and bracing the cracked framework sufficiently to make the ship navigable. Since no drydock was available, the most difficult and time-consuming job involved the severely damaged rudder, which extended far beneath the surface. A huge caisson had to be built on shore, then launched and fixed to the ship's stern so closely that the water could be pumped out and the work done in dry space beneath water level. The men worked day and night, but two months later, on November 22, the German Naval War Staff in Germany received the report that "as a result of the successful midget submarine attack . . . the *Tirpitz* has been put out of action for months."

Not until April of 1944 was the "Lonely Queen of the North" able to move from her anchorage into Altafjord, where even at half-speed she proved to be shaky—a pathetic picture of her former self. In August and September, she was damaged again, this time by air attacks. In October, she steamed slowly south to Tromsö. By now the course of the war had turned against the Germans, and they planned to use the ship only as a land-based fortress. But on November 12, 1944, the RAF dealt her the *coup de grâce.*

Plane after plane rained armor-piercing bombs upon her, until she rolled over and revealed the deadly wound the midgets had inflicted in Kaafjord. The enormous hole in her bottom had been filled with hundreds of yards of reinforced concrete, but it symbolized the irreparable damage done to the frames in her hull from her port-side bow, where three of the X-craft bombs had exploded simultaneously, to her stern, where the fourth bomb had virtually destroyed her rudder. The X-craft attack had dealt her a fatal blow, and now, bearing out Doenitz's prophecy, she was finished.

It was not until after the war, when they were released and flown back to England, that the six survivors of Operation Source learned how successful their attack had been. Banner headlines proclaimed their return, and they were summoned to Buckingham Palace to be decorated. Although four hundred other men, from all the British services, were there as well, King George VI wanted to see the X-craft men first. Before presenting the awards, he stopped to speak to each.

"Good show," said the King. "Good show."

It was a proud moment for the survivors of the X-craft, but the words they prized above all came in 1948, when the British Admiralty issued an official report on their mission. "It is clear," it read in part, "that courage and enterprise of the highest order were shown by these gallant gentlemen, whose daring attack will surely go down in history as one of the most courageous acts of all time."

Index